DELIGHTING in

wisdom on the walk

compiled by

lori l. dixon Ed.S.

featuring

ELISE ANTHONY • JENNIFER LUNA
EMILY SCHWINDLER • DOROTHEA SHIELDS
DR. LYNNETTE SIMM • CONNIE WALLACE

dedication

I dedicate this book and these chapters to the women seeking more JOY in their lives. Let them see your light burning brightly in these women who have shared their own walk with you.

contents

introduction

Lori L. Dixon, Ed.S.

Welcome to the fifth divinely-inspired and curated book in the *Wisdom on the Walk* series. When the Lord gave me the new word for this edition, I was elated—and came to understand the "why" He felt the time was appropriate for this focus.

The word was DELIGHTING. I couldn't help but smile when I shared this opportunity for new and even seasoned authors to come and join us—asking them to craft an experience when the Lord's voice and wisdom in His word provided the joy, delight, and eventually rejoicing through the difficulty in their lives.

Six faithful women spoke a resounding *yes,* and we started this journey together. Little did I know I would even dig deeper into scripture for answers to the JOY dilemma for many of those individuals who are challenged with finding and holding onto that sometimes fleeting word… JOY.

As a therapeutic coach and Christian publisher, I encounter men and women who are going through life's challenges, obstacles, and sometimes even traumas that have left them feeling less joy for certain. Walking with them through the valleys and scaling the mountains in their lives truly brings the glimmers of hope and faith through these times. I believe I am equipped by the Lord through, yes, education and experience—but even more in what He whispers in the quiet silences to share with others for their life.

In writing the introduction in this newest book, I felt drawn to examine the words of the divine authors that God gave the scriptures. We know the use of the words **joy**, **delighting**, and **rejoicing** are not fluffy emotions— they're **spiritual postures**, often forged *in the middle of pressure*, not through the absence of it.

Let's walk through these words in their **biblical meaning and context**, not just the modern "feel-good" versions. Just a little Bible study for you all.

Use your new ideas and insights to substitute in the writings of each woman as she gently and even sometimes stumbles, giving you the meanings of joy in her life. May this bless you even further in your reading and studying of the Word.

Joy (Hebrew: simchah | Greek: chara)

Joy in the Bible is rooted, not reactive.

What it really means:

- **Hebrew simchah** → gladness that flows from *being aligned with God*

- **Greek chara** → a settled gladness anchored in grace

Joy is **covenantal**. It's not dependent on circumstances—it's a response to **who God is and what He has promised**.

> The joy of the LORD is your strength.
>
> Nehemiah 8:10, NIV

Biblical *Context:* Israel had just returned from exile. They were hearing the Law read aloud and were **weeping** because they realized how far they had fallen. Nehemiah tells them:

This is not a day for sorrow—this is a day for joy.

Joy here is **restoration joy**—the strength that comes from being brought back into the right relationship.

> Though you have not seen Him, you love Him… you rejoice with joy inexpressible.
>
> 1 Peter 1:8, NASB

Biblical *Context:* Written to persecuted believers. No comfort. No ease. Joy is **supernatural evidence of faith**, not emotional denial.

Biblical Joy = confidence in God's nearness and faithfulness.

Take time here to reflect. Ground your thoughts.

Delighting   (Hebrew: Chāphets / ʿĀnag **)**

Delight is desire turned Godward.

What it really means:

- Chāphets → to take pleasure in, to desire deeply
- ʿĀnag → to be soft, pliable, luxuriating in God's presence

Delighting is **intentional affection**. You choose what you delight in—and Scripture is clear that *what you delight in shapes your life.*

> Delight yourself in the LORD, and He will give you the desires of your heart.
>
> Psalm 37:4, NASB

This psalm contrasts the **wicked who prosper quickly** with the righteous who wait. Delight is an *act of trust*, not a transaction.

God doesn't give you *whatever* you want—He **reshapes your desires** as you delight in Him.

> His delight is in the law of the LORD.
>
> Psalm 1:2, NASB

Psalm 1 is the *gateway to all Psalms*. It establishes that flourishing comes from **loving God's ways**, not merely obeying them.

Delight = loving what God loves

Take time here to reflect. Ground your thoughts.

Rejoicing   (**Hebrew:** Rānan / Gîl | **Greek:** Chairō)

Rejoicing is joy expressed out loud and outward.

What it really means:

- Rānan → to shout, sing, cry out with joy
- Gîl → to spin, leap, exult
- Chairō → to actively celebrate

Rejoicing is **joy made visible**. It is often commanded in Scripture—not because it's easy, but because it's **formative**.

> Rejoice in the LORD always. Again I say, rejoice.
>
> Philippians 4:4, KJV

Paul wrote this **from prison**. This is not denial—this is **defiance**.

Rejoicing declares: *God is still God here.*

> This is the day which the LORD has made; let us rejoice and be glad in it.
>
> Psalm 118:24, NASB

A psalm sung during **Passover**, pointing forward to deliverance—ultimately fulfilled in Christ.

Rejoicing is often **prophetic**—celebrating what God is doing *before* it's fully seen.

Take time here to reflect. Ground your thoughts.

Think of them like this:

- **Delight** is the *root* (what you love)
- **Joy** is the *fruit* (what you carry)
- **Rejoicing** is the *expression* (what you release)

You can **choose delight**. Joy is **produced by the Spirit**. Rejoicing is **obedient expression**.

Where right now is God inviting you:

- to **delight** again (affection),
- to **receive joy** again (strength),
- or to **rejoice** again (expression)?

As you begin to read each story written by these precious women, see if they are delighting, are carrying joy or finding it, or rejoicing in their walk with the Lord's wisdom. After each chapter there will be reflection pages, scripture mapping specifically important to their story, and pictures to inspire you.

Join us, won't you?

joy in our calling

Lori L. Dixon, Ed.S.

There is a quiet joy that lives inside a calling. It is not always loud. It does not always appear as excitement or ease. Sometimes it is simply the deep knowing that the path beneath your feet was placed there by God Himself.

Many women begin their calling with passion and vision, yet somewhere along the journey, the weight of responsibility, uncertainty, or delay can cause joy to fade into duty.

The assignment remains, but the delight feels distant.

Yet Scripture reminds us that joy was never meant to come from outcomes alone. Joy is rooted in the One who calls, equips, and walks with us through every step of obedience.

When God invites us into a work—whether ministry, leadership, writing, mentoring, or building something that blesses others—He never intended the journey to be carried by striving alone. His joy becomes the strength that steadies us when the work grows heavy and the courage that reminds us why we began.

The calling may stretch us. It may refine us. At times it may even break open places in our hearts we did not know needed healing. Yet within the sacred work God assigns, He also plants the grace to continue and the joy that renews our strength.

Joy in our calling is not the absence of struggle. It is the presence of God within the work.

And when we learn to delight in Him again, the work becomes more than an assignment—it becomes worship.

What experiences and memories does this reveal in your life?

I know my deepest and most impactful one…

In my early middle school years, I began my favorite activity… going to church camp. I loved the relationships I made, learning more about the Lord and strengthening my faith, and being in nature.

This particular year, I was growing in my ability to lead a devotional for our group each day. At that time in my life,

I wrestled with some school friendships that were shifting and the feeling of loss in what we had together at that age was difficult. In my prayer time, the Lord sent me to Psalms 30:5b, "Weeping may endure for the night, but joy comes in the morning" (AMP).

He heard me.

He heard my tears and even collected them because they matter to Him.

I heard, I am HIS child.

My young teen's tears and thinking *do* matter.

I wasn't dismissed; I was heard.

I'm still heard. All the adult tears over pain, loss, difficulty, betrayal, and death…I am heard and I am still His child.

So are YOU.

AND… after those tears, He promises us JOY!

We know our calling was placed within us at birth. It is our DNA and still we struggle and we doubt that we even have one specially made for us. The Lord reminds us the source of our JOY is in our calling and our identity in our Heavenly Father. It is larger than our assignments on earth. Those are how we use our calling the Father has instilled to further His Kingdom on earth and to assist us in influencing and impacting others to know Him.

> The joy of the LORD is your strength.
> Nehemiah 8:10, NIV

In my therapeutic work, I have encountered many times the individual who has not felt joy. Sometimes they remember being young and feeling that inner joy, but lost it along the path of their life. They ask me, *"How do I get it back?"*

That question can be simple—let's go to the Lord and renew that from where it all began. We also talk about how the world can diminish our joy in life through comparison, delayed feelings of inadequacy and lack, over-responsibilities that have been placed on us due to circumstance, work or even ministry fatigue, and carrying outcomes or desires instead of obedience in the walk God has created for us.

Paul writes in the letter to the Galatians 5:22, as he shares the fruits of the Holy Spirit produced within us "is divine love in all its varied expressions, joy that overflows, peace that subdues, patience that endures, kindness in action, a life full of virtue, faith that prevails, gentleness of heart, and strength of spirit. Never set the law above these qualities, for they are meant to be limitless" (Galatians 5:22–23, TPT).

God placed those qualities within us and the Holy Spirit activates them to be felt and shared with others in all we do. We don't need to find joy; we need to remember how to activate it.

Reflection: How will you follow the path of the Lord in your life and remain faithful instead of believing you must be successful instead of joyful?

Whenever I heard the scriptures that included the word "delighting," I felt it was an inward emotional connection to the Lord. Just like a gentle hug or a tender hand on my shoulder. As we walk in our calling and learn to make adjustments and listen to the voice of God in it all, He shifts our focus from our acceptance and performance which resides in the world to relishing in His presence and peace.

It is the true delight we experience when our own desires align with the purpose He has placed within us. More than joy, it is internal ease and calmness in Him. I believe in that moment, we remember what it was like to be in Heaven and be in His fatherly presence.

For those who had a loving father on this earth, the concept may be easier. For others who have felt loss or lack of an influence, they may go through experiences to learn about the many ways our Heavenly Father shows us what ultimate and complete love feels like in our lives.

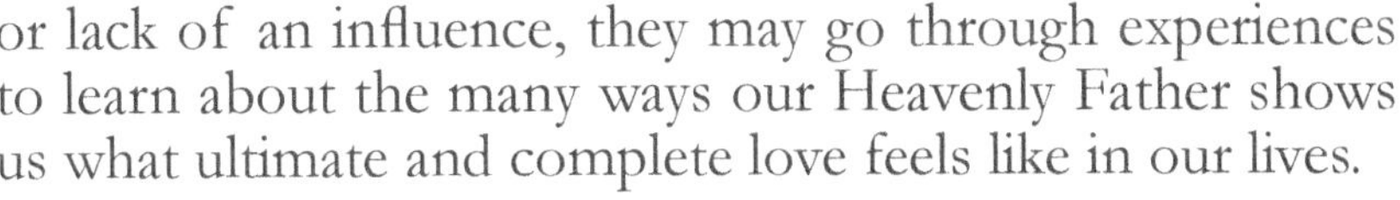

The very essence of God brings forth many images for Him; the healer, the listener, the disciplinarian, the strong tower, and the problem-solver. These are only examples you may yourself have felt from your relationship with Him. Yet, feeling such tangible truths is the pure joy and honoring we can sense and hold tight.

In Psalm 37:3–5, King David shares his poetic praise for the wisdom the Lord had given Him. See if this resonates in your own life:

"Keep trusting in the Lord and do what is right in His eyes. Fix your heart on the promises of God, and you will dwell in the land, feasting on His faithfulness. Find your delight and true pleasure in Yahweh, and he will give you what you desire most. Give God the right to direct your life, and as you trust Him along the way, you'll find He pulled it off perfectly" (TPT).

Delight restores **holy motivation**. Find the delight in your life and allow the Lord to be your guide as He navigates your steps.

Joy and delighting are two profound and complex words, or so we may feel. Reading them within the context of the Holy Scriptures provides direction and understanding for all of us.

The Lord asks us to worship and rejoice in Him even before our prayers or "harvest moments" are revealed. Remaining in gratitude and pure joy in Him, is an act of faith and belief in His desire to care for us, His children.

When we praise Him even in our difficulties and trials, it creates a mindset shift in perspective from striving to thriving and trusting. As we rejoice in our work and life each day, it sanctifies our actions and honors the Lord in it all. Almost as if you are dedicating your daily tasks to Him. It lifts it higher in our own perspective and especially in the Lord's.

> Be cheerful with joyous celebration in every season of life. Let your joy overflow! And let gentleness be seen in every relationship for the Lord is ever near.
>
> Philippians 4:4–5, TPT

Our calling is in all we do. Joy becomes a mindset shift and brings the elevating of our work to honor Him.

Reflection: What mundane tasks can you lift for the Lord and see His hand in it all? You can be a conduit of joy and rejoicing. How can we explain that to our children and to others?

The path we walk for our calling is not promised to be easy—but we are promised that God will never leave or forsake us. When we take steps in the "valley" of life with joy, it renews our endurance. Joy does protect our heart as we may struggle with stress, burnout, and negative influences around us. If we focus on the work and how it belongs to God and the why of the journey, we flourish and walk *renewed.*

God bolsters in us what He assigns. He doesn't give us the work and not prepare us, nor leave us while we are enduring the struggles of life. In Isaiah 4:31, we know that "those that wait for the Lord, [who expect, look for, and hope in Him] will gain new strength and renew their power; They will lift up their wings [and rise up close to God] like eagles [rising toward the sun]; They will run and not become weary; They will walk and not grow tired" (Isaiah 40:31, AMP).

It is refreshing and renewing for us to know that God ordained our calling and the exact needs we will require. He understands how difficult the path will be. *He sustains what He assigns.* Does that feel significant to know and understand?

When the Lord asked me to create the *Wisdom on the Walk* books and then to invite other women to join me, I had no idea what He would be designing and fostering within each of us. I've cried with these women, laughed, protected their wounds, and lifted all to the Lord.

That is why our stories and actions matter! They are significant in our lives and as we heal and transform into where God is sending us; other women heal and are lifted higher as we rejoice in them. That's the **WoW** in action.

Remember our JOY of the calling in all is profound. It guides our Christian walk.

Remember your "yes" moments with God.

Reconnect with your purpose daily behind the work He gives you.

Release outcomes we receive with gratitude and share them.

Rejoice in the small steps of obedience you take. Each one a simple, yet profound dedication to the Lord.

Reminders in the holy scriptures:

So now, what can I ever give back to God to repay Him for the blessings He's poured out on me? I will lift up His cup of salvation and praise Him extravagantly for all He's done for me. I will fulfill the promise I made to God in the presence of His gathered people (Psalm 116:12–14, TPT).

"This is the very day of the Lord that brings gladness and joy, filling our hearts with glee. O God, please come and save us again; bring us your breakthrough victory!" (Psalm 118:24, TPT).

Before the fruit appears…

before the work is finished…

before others recognize what God is doing…

Joy quietly asks one question:

Will you still say yes?

And when we do, the work becomes lighter, the heart becomes steadier, and the calling once again becomes a place where we walk with God.

> "Though you have not seen Him, you love Him… you rejoice with joy inexpressible."
>
> 1 Peter 1:8, NASB

Prayer to God

Lord, I seek you to assist the woman reading these stories to find her calling in You and fill her life with inexplicable JOY. Let her touch others' lives in her journey of faith and belief in You! Let us resonate for joy and delight in our lives with the light of Your Son, Jesus Christ.

Amen.

Reflection

Do you remember when God first stirred the calling inside of you?

What is the identity in the Lord at this time? What is He working on in you? How is He showing up to direct your steps?

deepening your walk

Scripture Verse

Translations

Key Words

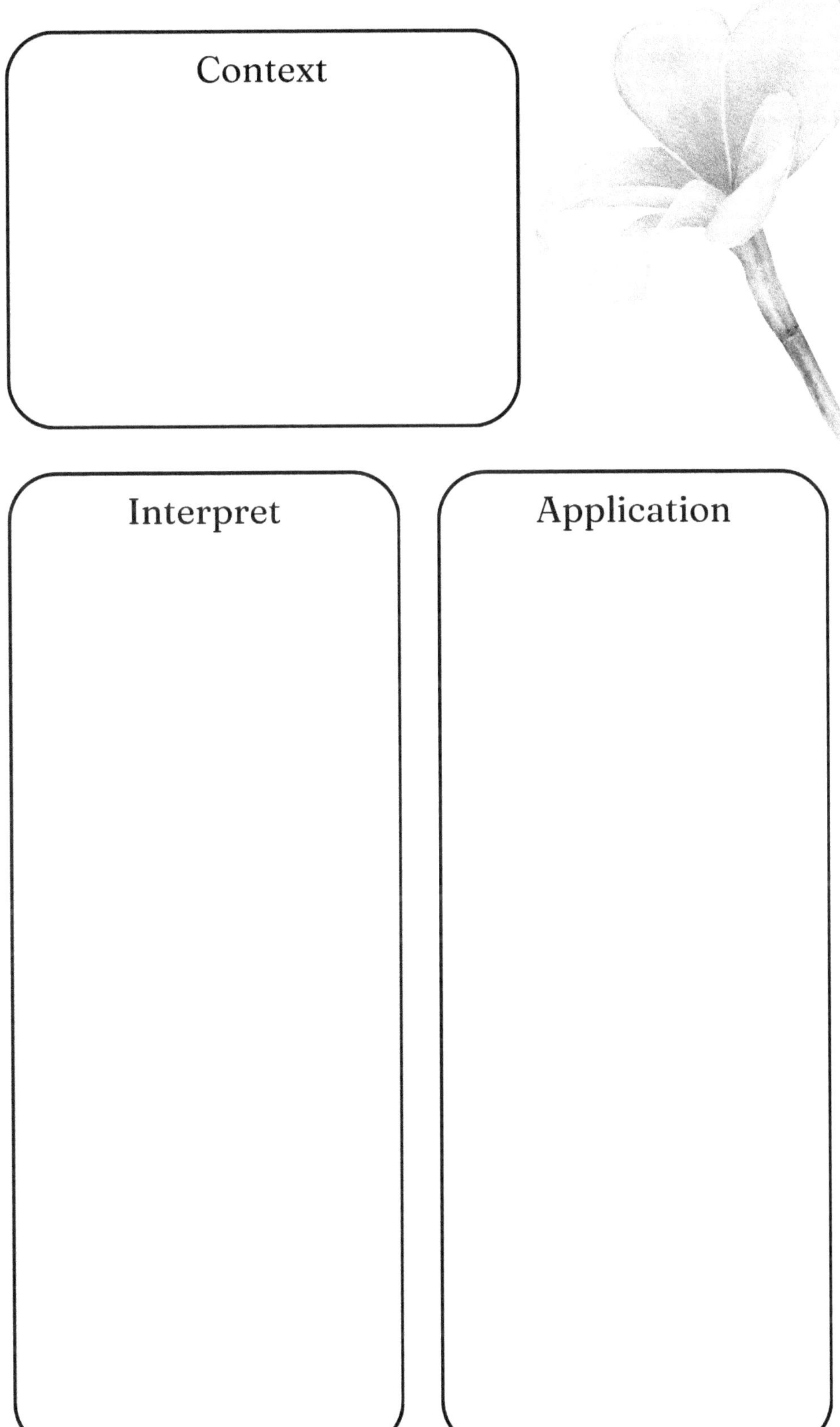
Context

Interpret

Application

the great design

Emily Schwindler

It was a crisp December day. The type of lazy Sunday just after Thanksgiving that presents itself to be the perfect, glittering day for decorating the house for Christmas. The family was all abuzz as boxes and favorite treasured items began to emerge.

Grandpa was having a long winter's nap, while the rest of us decided to put on a new cassette tape of Christmas songs sung by Bing Crosby. Bing's voice was very similar to Grandpa's, so we knew he would love to hear the carols as he drifted in and out. In fact, the tape was meant to be a Christmas present for him, but we couldn't wait to share the music, as it perfectly accentuated the moment. We listened to it all day—flipping the clunky tape over and pressing play with all our might when one side ended.

The prized nativity was constructed on the mantel just as it had been purchased, piece by fragile piece. The delicate display was an Italian porcelain set that Grandpa believed was a testimony in itself. He was so proud that people visiting the parsonage might see the intricate scene and be moved to feel the story of Christ's birth anew. He purchased the set one character at a time because the 99-cent price tag of each was a hefty sum on a preacher's salary. That golden day, it was being cherished by its third generation of owners as my sisters and I carefully unwrapped each figure—so perhaps Grandpa was on to something.

We danced around, joyfully going about our work, and breaks were taken for turkey sandwiches and hot chocolate. The chill of the day was forgotten as the warmth of family and the illuminated memories of the past filled our day with happiness. We sang along to *White Christmas* and began to imagine our requests for Santa.

The tree and the garlands were put out with care, adorned with bells that softly tinkled carols and glowing bubble lights that fascinated the eye. Grandpa delighted in hearing us all chatting and singing, even more so now because his sight had left him due to complications from his diabetes. His health decline led him to retirement from ministry, and for he and Grandma to move in with their daughter and three granddaughters. Our home was a comfortable refuge where we leaned on one another during this time that required extra support and care.

We lived in the ranch house with shiny wood floors and a large corner lot for a little over a year, and settled into our routines in our multi-generational home of joy and togetherness.

However, there was an extra layer of true anticipation that shone out that Sunday. The hope of the Christmas season bloomed brightly against the cold like a brilliant winter poinsettia.

And it was on that very luminous afternoon that Grandpa opened his blind eyes and exclaimed, "Angels, Angels!" and passed away.

We buried Grandpa on Wednesday. Less than 24 hours later, homemade, hand-decorated gingerbread cookies showed up at my school to share with friends—it was my birthday.

I'll never forget those gingerbread cookies. They had red hots and white icing decorations. It was a sophisticated recipe to share with the palette of a seven-year-old, but it was the traditional family recipe that had been salvaged from a tattered Martha Stewart magazine. I remember feeling grateful that my birthday wasn't forgotten, but also conflicted at the empty chair next to mine at the dinner table that evening.

Now I see those cookies— and that week—as so much more. Our household was now touched by grief. It hung around the rooms like heavy air that pushes in on you. I felt his loss every day. He was a part of everything, and now there was nothing of him left. His body, his clothes, his chair—all whisked away. Nothing left but our sadness and memories.

In that era of life, I couldn't understand my grandmother's loss. I saw it in her eyes and heard it in her muffled sobs, but seeing and hearing aren't the same as truly understanding. The easy childhood moments for me were filled with the brilliance of ignorance. I can see that now.

Those early days after her husband died, Grandma still made meals, we had clean clothes, and there was Christmas dinner on the table. To me, everything was still covered in the sheen of childhood happiness.

But I did start to pick up on the grief and joy that were now inextricably mixed together for her: the accidental miscount of plates for a celebration dinner, the smiles that never reached her eyes, and the tears that flowed during certain hymns at church. Even seeing these things did not equate to deeply understanding them. I was living my pure, child moments and she was living her complex, grey adult moments.

After losing her husband of 42 years, my grandmother was understandably lost in grief. I remember her crying during the day and listening to his voice on old, crackling recordings for comfort. She kept her routine, going through the motions every day. Getting up, reading her Bible, taking care of us, and collapsing into bed at night. She did that every day until she could do more. She slowly found her way anew. Never the same and never back to normal, but she did find herself through the daily grounding of being the hands and feet of God, serving others around her.

In fact, this was a pattern she had adopted over a lifetime. When she felt lonely as a young wife whose husband was often away on church business visiting sick beds or at seminary, she channeled her loneliness into making baby quilts for mothers in her congregation to hold in the lonely hours of motherhood. When she was sorrowful, she helped the grieving by serving at the funeral luncheons or driving widows to doctor appointments. When she was tired, she gave a place of rest to others in the simple comforts of a clean house, fresh sheets, and homemade dinners. When she needed community, she taught Sunday school, made pies for the bake sale, and organized the family reunions.

As Grandmother moved through her days, she always instructed us to follow her example and pray without ceasing. Her petitions to the Lord were great and small. They had a constant dialogue filled with gratitude, humility, and wonder. This attitude of putting her face to the sun and letting the shadows fall behind her always reminded me of the instructions in Philippians 4, verse 8: "Finally, brothers and sisters, whatever is true, whatever is noble, whatever is right, whatever is pure, whatever is lovely, whatever is admirable—if anything is excellent or praiseworthy—think about such things."

It was always an honor, therefore, when she would say we were, "cut from the same cloth." But a better phrase for our relationship would never compare to that perfect phrasing. We were made of the same thing. She understood my heart and poured into my soul all manner of loving-kindness and grace.

In fact, she didn't just understand my heart; it was more like we shared a heart. A heart for serving others. When things get difficult, we are the type to dig into the now. We feel the needs of others and answer the call. Grandma's gift of peace and presence blessed everyone she met. You could feel the calm all around her and know the love of God by looking in her eyes. She gave and gave. Everything God gave her, she gave away. And she was always assured through faith He would somehow refill her cup.

A perfect example would be "our" quilt. I never thought we would actually finish it. It took ages (in the eyes of a teenager). The log cabin pattern required innumerable strips of fabric of different sizes and different patterns. She had scraps of fabric from every project she ever started and every person who ever offered her bits of their stockpiles. And, being the unique person she was, she looked at that cabinet of mismatched mess and thought it might be the perfect next project. She assured me that what mattered was how all that random jumble was put together.

Every day after school, I would help. Gran cut strips in the right lengths throughout the day, and we would piece them together at night. The random rectangles were laid on the floor of the formal living room. The oriental rug was long forgotten under the critical mass of piles arranged by size and general color. She would call for me to bring pieces of a certain length and shade (light or dark), and I would run them to her as she stitched them on the sewing machine in the other room. The hum of the machine kept the rhythm as I made the many journeys back and forth.

At first, it didn't look like anything. To me, the different patterns and sizes appeared completely chaotic. I just couldn't imagine how all those people's junk was going to become something of value. But then, as we fit them all together, blocks took form. Then there were squares. Finally, when we stepped back, I could understand what she had known all along: there was a grand design and so much beauty in all those unwanted, mismatched fragments.

After piecing, the quilting began. Stitch after tiny stitch, it was a job that seemed impossible. Grandma poured her lonely hours into this beautiful work of art. Each stitch another tick of the clock. It was draped over her day and night with the large hoop holding the fabric in place as she worked over each sliver with love. It was truly her masterful attention to each piece that made it all cohesive. She had faith (and experience), which taught her that each quarter inch was progress. Even small steps are steps.

That quilt was intended to be a gift for someone, but after the countless hours spent together, I asked if it wasn't now "our" quilt, and she had to agree. She showed me through quiet perseverance how love can transform shredded, forgotten nothings into something magnificent. We took a photo proudly holding our finished product, and that quilt is still my prized possession.

It is no surprise that when I had dark and difficult times, my grandmother was the person I would trust to sit with me in my hardship. She did not try to fix anything or make it disappear. She supported me so I could fall apart. When I wronged her, she reminded me we are called to forgive (Matthew 18: 21–22). When I felt like giving up, she reminded me to lean on a rock that is stronger (Psalm 61: 2–3). When it all felt too much, she instructed me to take the yoke that is easy (Matthew 11: 28–30).

It was in the small moments she showed me how to listen to and follow God and how to love others without expectations. Her love revealed itself slowly in acts of service. She made me jackets and Brownie Scout uniforms when money was tight so I wouldn't go without. She remembered all my friends' names. She knew every wish of my heart and held me in her arms when I asked how I could give my life to Christ.

But I also saw this in Grandma's interactions with others. People would always share unprompted, personal things with her. Whether it was the teller at the bank, the man at the post office, or the person walking by, people naturally opened up to her. She was a safe place and a quilter of life. Whatever scraps people offered, she cared about deeply and understood their uniqueness. She showed them love and compassion, stitching their words into something more.

When I started my career in deathcare, we spoke on the phone every day on my hour-long commute about the many experiences I was having, stories and traditions I was learning, and families I was serving. She prayed for all of them. From the unborn child to the 102-year-old—and always for me. And I would never have had the strength to serve them without her prayers always lifting me. It was then I started to notice I had the same ability of receiving people's unprompted truths.

I'd like to think that through this receiving of their stories of loss and grief, I have also taken up a complimentary role: a quilter of death. Each story, each family, each pain—a scrap of their memories shared with me. I strive to receive them with love and compassion, as Grandma did.

In our daily talks, I would share my stories of loss and Gran would share her experiences of love, still forever crafting our log cabin design. She was the constant thread through my years, the love of one tiny stitch of time after another. Together, we didn't so much make sense of the world, but we learned to embrace life's ups and downs by knowing God held us through it all. The darkness didn't get lighter nor the light dimmer—it simply revealed itself to all fit into a greater design. The joys and struggles of life existing together and enriching one another.

Gran began losing her memories in her latter years. I could feel the solid ground shifting slowly under our feet. Like grains of sand that were too small to notice at first, but eventually moving in earnest. But in this time when the colors of her memory began to change, a beautiful thing happened. The smiles reached her eyes again. Her moments were no longer plagued by ghosts of the past. The light in her day was no longer dimmed by pain and loss. The pall of memories was lifted and her joy radiated.

Yet, the darkness did not disappear. It was only transferred. Now I was the one who knew the truth, saw each shadowy moment for what it lacked. Every candle casts a shadow. For me, each new memory became a mix of the joy of the now with the sorrow of all it was not. I finally and deeply understood the experience of holding both truths at once.

We still had a bond so strong she would always recognize herself in me. Even when she finally forgot my name, we were woven together by something more eternal. After all, two pieces of the same cloth do not need names to know they belong to one another.

She died on a crisp Sunday in February. Her last words were as equally moving of a testimony as her husband's had been. On that overcast day, we lay in her bed together. She reached her arms into the air and asked her Father to pick her up.

We buried her next to the love of her life on a Wednesday. Then I made Valentines for my child's school party, and I completely understood why gingerbread cookies taste like love to me.

And how do we see it all and make sense of any of it? My answer is love. 1 John 4:16 tells us, "And so we know and rely on the love God has for us. God is love. Whoever lives in love lives in God, and God in them." The quilters stitch it all together and make something beautiful from all the broken pieces. We need both the light and the dark for perspective and inspiration. It is essential as one reveals the other in time.

She revealed—through how she lived her life—a never-ending project. When life stops making sense, our quilt helps me remember my work is far from finished. It takes hundreds of pieces of all sizes, being cared for one-by-one to make the beauty appear, but once you finally see—and really understand—you can have confidence that it all fits together somehow.

As the years pass and my understanding grows, I cherish each person I am blessed to care for in my work with the dead. I see them as each of God's masterpieces. Some are stories of struggle, others of triumph. Some are tales told in minutes and some unfold over a century. Some are beautiful, epic goodbyes and some are tragically heartbreaking. Different lengths, different patterns, and different shades—they are all important.

They endure in the stories and memories their loved ones carry and in the scraps they choose to share with the rest of us. And when all our memories fade, the quilt will remain, for God has a memory all His own that endures forever (Malachi 3:16).

At this stage of life, I have collected enough pieces to know the truth I couldn't understand as a child. Experiencing pure joy as an adult means acknowledging sadness alongside it. And even though we might never view the world through the bright, joyful ignorance of childhood again, we can choose to see that the introduction of darkness, pain, and loss makes joy shine out even

more brilliantly in contrast. We can open our blind eyes, outstretch our arms faithfully on a cloudy day, and experience the loving embrace just waiting to be known.

What countless conversations with my grandmother, seeing death daily, and trying to make sense of it all has taught me is to fully open myself to experience life's highs and lows. When I acknowledged the duality of love and loss, I finally understood what each had to teach me. I choose to embrace both truths, delight in what each reveals, and continue to serve others with a joyful heart.

Now I am the one nurturing the younger generation as a mother and church school helper. I am comforting the widows and praying for others. I make the pies she taught me to make, and lead my daughter's Girl Scout Troop, encouraging them to be kind and patient. Everything she gave to me, I have cherished, internalized, and used as my foundation in Christ. She demonstrated what it means to show others the love of God through delighting in daily acts of service.

My email signature line includes this quote from Mother Teresa: "Not all of us can do great things. But we can do small things with great love." I know I will never be famous or change the world, but I have a wonderful example of how love applied to life can change everything. So I encourage you to live your piece fully and joyfully, with the knowledge that it is important to the great design, and to God, and to all the quilters of this world.

My deepest thanks go to my husband and children who have shown unwavering support and love as I pursue my dreams. Without you, I could not have made it this far. I send my heartfelt appreciation to my sisters who believed in me and saw me through the moments that might have broken me. I feel forever grateful for Lois who never got to write her book. May she know her dreams keep me moving forward, and her love and prayers will sustain me forever.

Finally, to all the holy souls who I have had the privilege of providing assistance, thank you for allowing me to be a small part of your final earthly chapter.

Prayer to God

Eternal God,

The heaviness of loss and daily commitments can feel overwhelming at times. Help us to know the refreshment that comes from washing the feet of others—just as Jesus did in the midst of accepting his own path to the cross.

Thank you for showing us an example of quiet servitude and love so we can trust we are doing enough. Your son's sacrifice was not a loud, clambering explosion. Rather, it was a quiet dignity in the face of oppression, a loving act that has reverberated for thousands of years.

Help us to remember there is power in humbly serving and loving others—just as Jesus did. When we face life's challenges, grief, and setbacks, let us look to our left and right and focus on what we can do to make a difference today. Help us to be the hands and feet of God for one another and find delight in making one another's burdens lighter.

Amen.

Reflection

How is God calling you to serve others?

Reflect on a dark time in your life. What light moments did you experience during the darkness? How can you see God stitching both together in your life?

Where do I start? You were a piece of my heart.

You stitched our lives together
and taught me to do the same.
Until those skills became a tether,
a bond too strong to name.

Quilting scraps of memory
each day adding more.
A beautiful patchwork history
of facts infused with lore.

We built our log cabin
adding our dark and our light.
We trusted the pattern would happen
by including both wrong and right.

You trusted the process.
You knew where we would be.
I never had to guess
or even look up and see.

But now the quilt is finished
and your stead presence gone.
Somehow its glimmer diminished
in the light of this new dawn.

I'll wrap it close around me
and remember how you chose
to stitch us together daily
even before I arose.

So I will keep on sewing
the story of us two
because as long as my blood is flowing
you are part of what I do.

—*Emily Schwiundler*

deepening your walk

Scripture Verse

Translations

Key Words

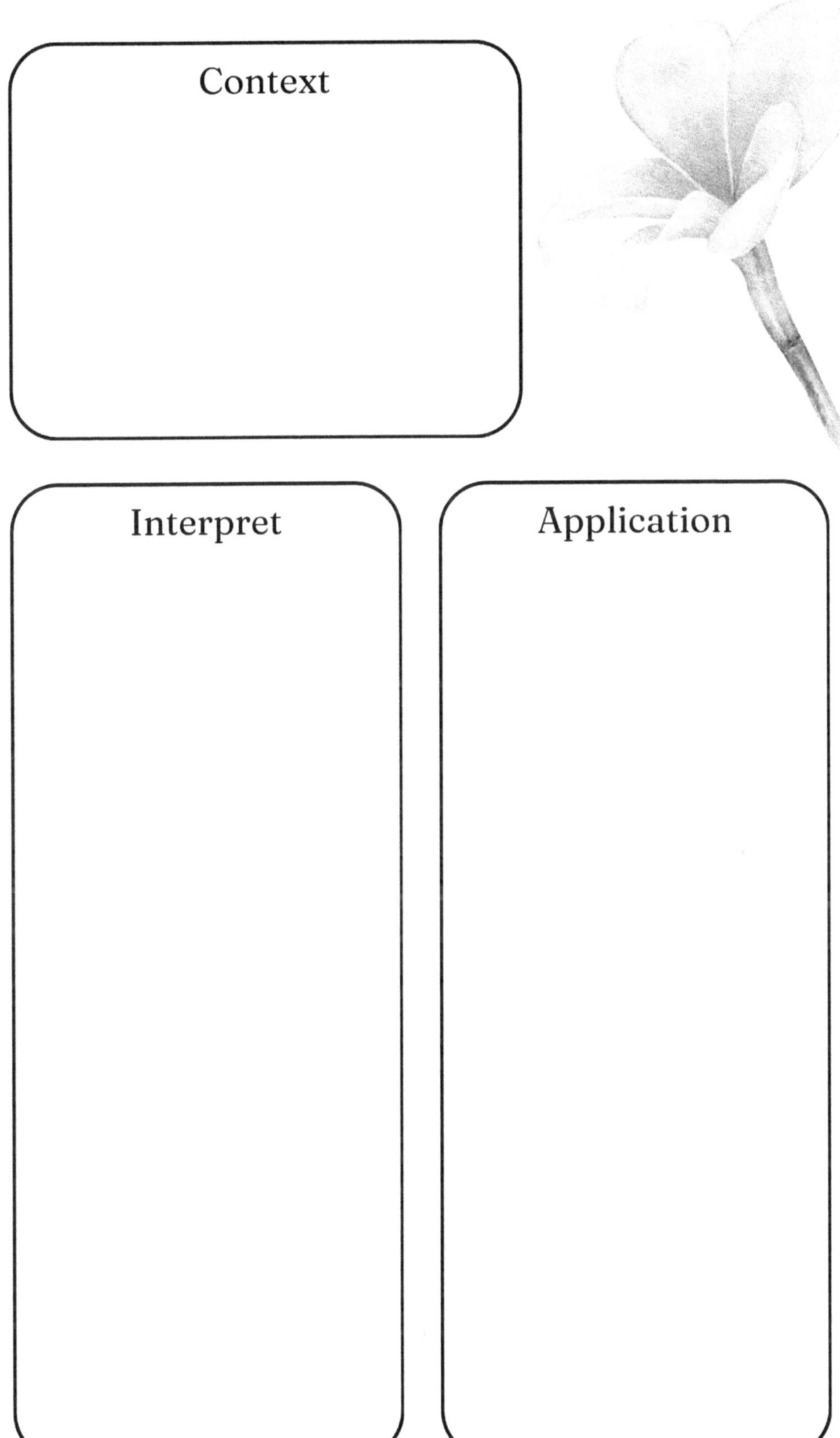

Context

Interpret

Application

leading with joy—even when it's not easy

Jennifer Luna

> For the Lord your God is a merciful God; He will not abandon or destroy you or forget the covenant with your ancestors, which He confirmed to them by oath.

Deuteronomy 4:31, NIV

> The Lord our God has blessed us, and so now there are as many of us as there are stars in the sky.

Deuteronomy 1:10. NIV

> "Faith, salvation, the word, and prayer are the weapons of our warfare."

Voddie Baucham

No one can be that happy ALL the time.

The whisper arrives softly—almost harmless—yet heavy enough to dim the room. In its presence, I begin to shrink. My eyes lower. My spirit retreats. I slip quietly into the background, choosing invisibility as refuge. Confrontation stirs but never rises. The heat in my body subsides. Autopilot takes over. The instinct to please replaces the courage to speak. Joy is pushed down, hidden, faded into the back—as though my light has learned when it is safer to go unseen.

Yet joy does not always arrive loudly. More often, it slips in quietly—through the smallest moments, through places we never imagined joy could enter. It lives in the ordinary, flickering through our daily lives like a steady flame. We catch glimpses of it, sometimes chase it, sometimes hold it briefly. And for some of us, it is taken just as quickly—snatched, shaken loose, wrenched away—leaving behind a quiet ache that whispers: you are unworthy, unseen, or easily forgotten.

This chapter is an invitation to return to JOY—directly from the source. Not as something to pursue or achieve, but as something to receive. To feel. To allow. To welcome and nurture, day by day, sometimes breath by breath. And when joy finds us—even for a moment—we are called to pause and recognize it for what it is: a lifeline from God. A reminder that we were never meant to shrink, fade, or disappear into the background, Stand firm, remain present, alive, and fully seen in the light each of us carry. We are all God's children, and each of us has something to offer the world and one another.

When we recognize joy as an extension of God and choose to delight in it, joy reveals itself not merely as a feeling, but as a path—a holy path. It unfolds with quiet wonder, leading us toward growth we did not plan and blessings we did not expect. As we lean into joy and share it freely, it gathers its family around us—gratitude, presence, and grace—lifting us out of the ordinary and awakening the gifts God has entrusted to us. Gifts waiting to be carried forward and released into the world.

Fast forward fifty years.

Scripture reminds us that God judges with perfect knowledge, accounting for the light each person has received, reserving final judgment for Himself alone—where even the hidden motives of the heart are revealed (Romans 1–2; 1 Corinthians 4:5). God alone knows.

> "I have given you this land… Now go in and take possession of the land the Lord swore He would give to your ancestors Abraham, Isaac, and Jacob."
>
> Deuteronomy 1:8, NIV

I turned fifty in March of 2024, something awakened in me—slowly, unmistakably. I felt a dehydration moving through my body, persistent and unresolved. I drank water, Gatorade, and even juice. Nothing satisfied the thirst.

I stopped. I listened. I breathed—four counts in, held for four, four counts out—and in the stillness, the truth met me: this was not physical. My spirit was parched. What I needed was not water from the earth, but water from heaven.

I felt it rise in my chest—my spirit reaching before my mind could catch up. God. The name startled me. I didn't go to church when I was a child. Did I even believe in God? And yet the longing was undeniable, reminiscing, of when my eldest daughter had planted the seed of us going to church many years ago and we three were baptized, but that was many moons ago. My thirst knew its source, even when I did not. I knew I needed water—God's water.

To receive it, I had to go backward before I could move forward—to remember who I am, who my people are, and the generations of faith, wounds, and grace still living within me, still calling me home.

Let the excavation begin.

My childhood returns in fragments, but one truth arises as a whole: I was raised in a home where joy was not occasional. It was ever-present—worn openly, practiced daily, offered freely to the world. Happiness faced forward, woven into the sacred rhythm of our family life.

And yet beneath that radiance flowed an unseen current—what my spirit now names PAIN. A parallel inheritance of survival, endurance, and unspoken suffering. Joy and pain did not cancel one another; they co-existed. Joy stood front-facing and visible, with a big, beautiful smile, while pain remained hidden in the depths of my family's spirit, carried quietly, faithfully, with resolve. Holding both required strength.

As I piece together my past, I saw how communities form lanes—unspoken but enforced. People learn where they belong, where they are permitted to stand. Over time, rules harden. Structure emerges. Control replaces care. Those who do not conform are cast out.

Even as a child, I felt it—the judgment, the lanes we were getting moved to, the expectations placed on me. I said no. This is not who I am. And my father would stop me gently but firmly: We don't talk back. We don't disrespect.

With time, I learned something deeper: some spirits may not know who they are, but they know who they are not. Stay in your lane. Hone your gift. Let God judge.

My parents carried love and joy in abundance. There was no church building, no formal doctrine. To this day, they apologize for that. I forgive them—just as I hope my children forgive me for what I did not yet know. What my parents could not see then, and only later understood, is this: though we did not attend church, Jesus was present in our home.

He lived in the lessons taught, the love given freely, the grace modeled daily. The Footprints poem hung in our home. I stood before it often, reading and allowing it to settle into my being, trying to understand how faith could carry someone when their own steps failed. While others were learning religion and enforcing lanes, unknowingly, we were learning how to walk with grace, every person and animal and even our Earth is worthy of respect, how to love without borders, how to trust we were never walking alone.

Choosing joy—holding space for pain without surrendering to it—required grit. It demanded spirit when surrender seemed easier, determination when joy was mistaken for weakness, and courage when authenticity carried a cost. This was not accidental happiness. It was forged.

What many mistook for ease was mettle—the strength to remain tender without breaking, to choose joy without blindness, and to stand firmly in one's own path while honoring the sacred ground of others.

Joy was never naïve. It took courage to choose light while fully aware of the darkness beneath it. Joy was not fragile—it was valor. A deliberate posture shaped by resolve.

As a child, I didn't fully understand my father's words—*"We are playing a different game."* I remember whispering under my breath, *"I think we're the only ones playing."*

Now I understand. We were playing a different game— one ruled not by fear or control, but by Joy rooted in faith, endurance, and love. Joy was not denial of pain; it was defiance of it. It was living water, sustaining us before we knew its name.

Fast forward to today.

> The LORD was angry with me because of you, and he solemnly swore that I would not cross the Jordan and enter the good land the Lord your God is giving you as your inheritance. I will die in this land; I will not cross the Jordan; but you are about to cross over and take possession of that good land. Be careful not to forget the covenant of the Lord your God that he made with you; do not make for yourselves an idol in the form of anything the Lord your God has forbidden.
>
> Deuteronomy 4:21–23, NIV

My spiritual walk deepened. I sought God intimately. I listened. I peeled layers of pain down to the bedrock of my spirit. The book of Deuteronomy keeps looping into and onto my path, I doubled down and listened to Deuteronomy on repeat beginning to end. Deuteronomy 4:22 attached itself to my spirit. I still don't know why that verse, but it makes me happy, I can do that—easy. Help others and my family cross into the good land, and if my fate is to die on this side, so be it, my mission will be completed, God willing.

Then the unthinkable happened.

About midway through my Earth year 2025, according to the police report, our youngest unalives herself. Forever twenty-seven. Rest in love and joy, Goodness. God willing we may see each other again. We love you.

When the call came, we shattered right along with her. We died that day, too. The pain was so unreal that, for me, the only way to keep being here on earth was to be angry; it was like the anger was keeping me from breaking. The pain was unbearable. Anger became the only thing holding us together. My flesh wanted to blame everyone and everything, especially myself. But anger cannot sustain a joyous spirit; I can hear and see my dad's face: *JOY is always front-face no matter.*

I had to just stop cold in my tracks, this you know, she loved Jesus. She loved people. She was filled with JOY and she shared her joy and

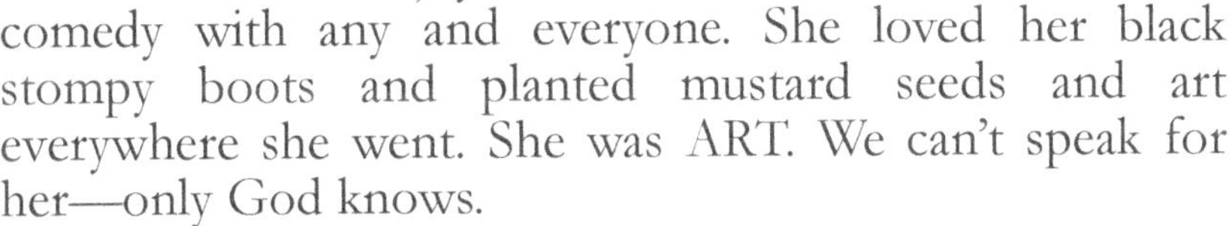

comedy with any and everyone. She loved her black stompy boots and planted mustard seeds and art everywhere she went. She was ART. We can't speak for her—only God knows.

I chose to release anger from my spirit. I began gathering what was shattered. In that broken space, I saw tears water the ground—I could see the seedlings of hope attracting butterflies and moths to rise and regrow all back together in the morning dew. I think back to all the times, conversations, dreams, and spaces we shared.

I choose JOY—not as denial, but as devotion. I carry her forward in how I love, how I make room for JOY, how I refuse to let anyone feel forgotten. Her mustard seeds took root in us, in me, in the lineage of JOY and courage passed hand to hand, heart to heart.

Grief broke the ground, but God met me there. From holy rupture, resolve rose.

Therefore, I urge you, brothers, in view of God's mercy, to offer your bodies as living sacrifices, hold and pleasing to God—This is your spiritual act of worship. Do not conform any longer to the pattern of this world, but be transformed into by the RENEWING OF YOUR MIND. Then you will be able to test and approve what God's will is—his good, pleasing and perfect will.

Romans 12:1-2, NIV

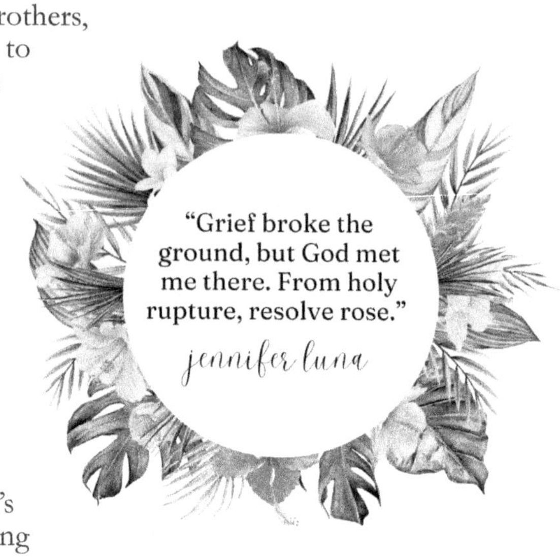

I stand now with Joy front-facing—anchored in faith, strengthened by lineage, and certain of this truth:

Love does not end.

Joy does not vanish.

What is planted in God is never lost.

I would like to end with this prayer:

"Father, we thank you and praise you for making us new creatures in Christ. Grant by your grace that we may walk in this newest of life. Grant that we might pursue the holiness and righteousness that is ours, in Christ. Grant that we might DELIGHT in the righteousness law of God as only those created in righteousness and holiness can. Grant that we might take every thought captive to the obedience of Christ. As only those who have been made new can, and grant that we will be more like Christ today than yesterday and more tomorrow than today.

This we pray in Christ name and sake. Amen."

Voddie Baucham

This chapter may be ending… but our story is far from over. Stories waiting to be told, and creativity unfolding in new ways. Stay tuned: a new book, documentary, and music are on the horizon. The journey continues.

"Stand firm, suffer well saints, may God continue to give us strength to endure."

Voddie Baucham

In honor of Samantha "Mantha~Vlad" Luna

Through healing, we honor life, love, and the family who remains

"We gave her wings; she taught us to fly"

Unknown

(Samantha wrote and gifted this poem to me)

To My Mother, 2013

If I could give my mom the world
Or anything she wanted,
I'd give her my own heart and soul
And leave my own heart haunted.
I'd take upon myself her life
With all its strife and pain,
And let her ease into some space
Where she could live again.
The pain for me would not be pain,
At least not for a while
For I'd be doing it for her,
And I would see her smile.
Yours the words that shaped my voice,
The spirit within mine,
Yours the will that shaped my choice,
My fortune, and my sign.
How lucky I was to have you
At the core of me!
Wise and good, you always knew
Just what I could be.
Happy Mother's Day

—*Samantha Luna*

My earthly father, thank you—and GrandMary—for walking in the ways of Jesus showing us what love truly looks like. Through your faith and example, you shaped both my life and my brother's. We carry your light with us always, grateful beyond words.

My earliest memory of loss is of my dear friend, Mary Helen Ferrer (May 13, 1974 – August 21, 1981). When third grade began, she was no longer there beside me. Mary Helen, I have carried your spirit with me through every season of my life.

At a crossroads in my life, I answered the call, serving two terms with AmeriCorps ARC NPC (2005-2007). One of the disasters we responded to was Hurricane Katrina alongside Lisa Tatum-Brown. Forever grateful our paths converged. Samantha never hesitated to serve—Her compassionate, driven spirit leaves a lasting imprint on all who truly knew her.

Mantha & MaM. Spring Break 2017—Mantha was so stoked for our UK adventure! God willing, we will one day continue our ever so awesome journeys again together.

deepening your walk

Scripture Verse

Translations

Key Words

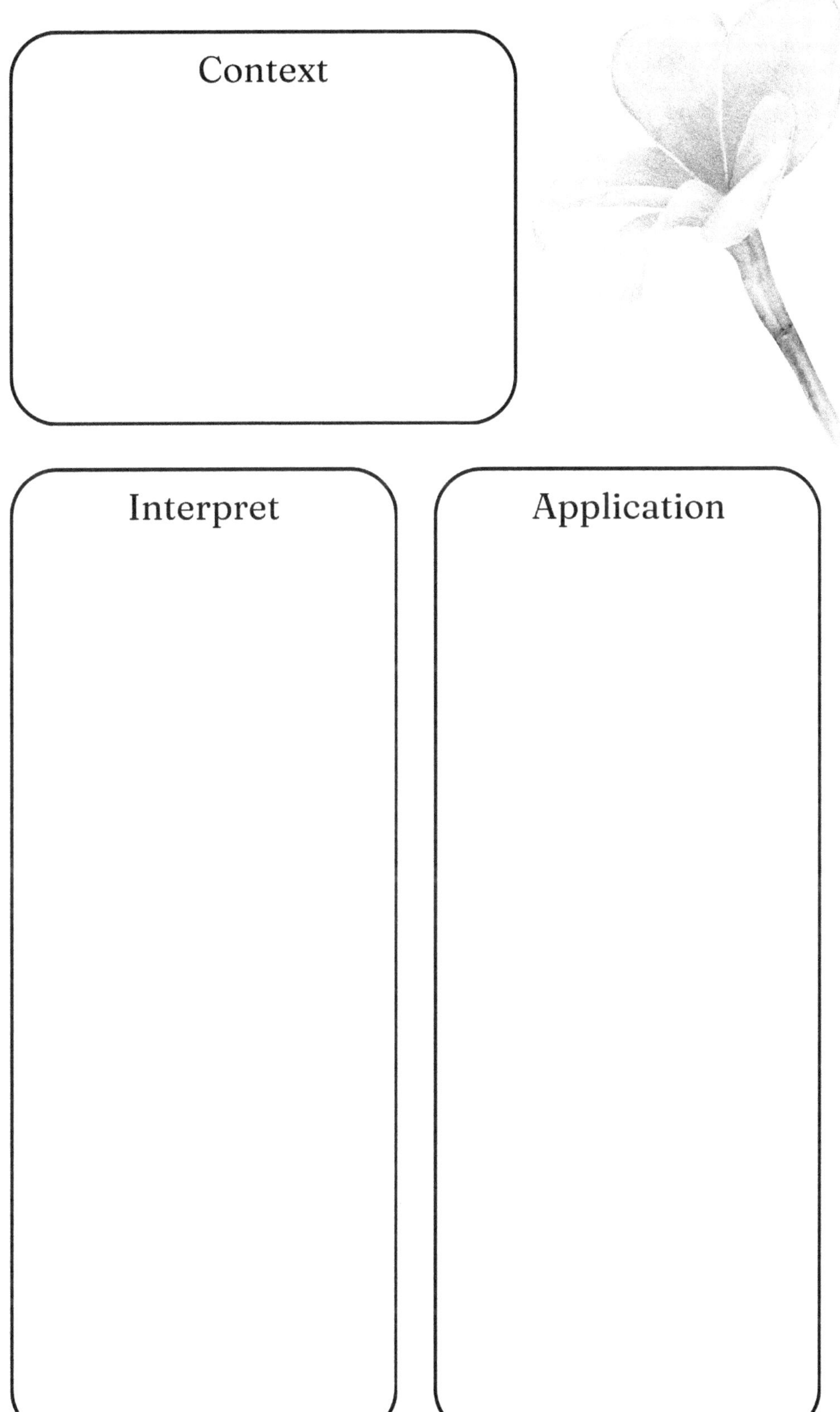

Context

Interpret

Application

BOUND

Bound
Bound in shame
By the things out of my control
Shame that shatters reality
Bound in shame for blame that was not mine to carry

Bound and wound
Up so tight that the tension
Became normal
Bound and wondering why I
Hold so much pain alone.

Bound so long it cracked my voice
The shell of me, only carrying the dust of who I was

Bound and becoming someone I don't know
Floating through life dazed & silent
Bound & broken by a man who took my choice

Bound & Brave
To speak my truth, bound & unbound
Breaking the chains that were never meant for me

Unbound by the sound
"You are never alone in Me"

Unbound by the sound
"You are never alone in Me"
Unbound in the word of truth,
I am unbound and I am enough

—Autumn Price

why is there a fly in my coffee?

Connie Wallace

The perfect cup of coffee. It tastes amazingly pure, totally clean, and seems to exude peace with every delicious sip. There it is… sitting on the picture-perfect table with the invitation to be lifted a few more times until all of its essence is consumed.

Honestly, it can be a truly spiritual experience, and it doesn't have to be coffee (if it's not your thing!). Just close your eyes and think of your favorite drink. Now take a deep breath, open your eyes, lift it to your mouth with the expectation of perfection and suddenly you realize… a common housefly is enjoying what should have been yours.

So often, life seems to be rocking along at a steady, no-or-low-drama pace. You seem to have the world by the tail, and you're so thankful for every breath. God has been good, and all the problems that others seem to encounter are not necessarily yours—or you haven't experienced them. You've never been there, so you can't truly identify. But you try; when a friend loses a father, a mother, another friend, a daughter, a son, a pet, a spouse, close family member—you do your best to support them with prayer and send words of comfort.

I was in this place for many years. My hard times were different. I hadn't experienced much loss, and life seemed to rock along mostly without devastation. Don't get me wrong, it wasn't always easy. My parents had their ups and downs, and there was never a shortage of knock-down drag-out fights in our household. But we knew how to love each other, even in the hardest times.

I grew up in a love-filled home with devoted parents and three warm-hearted siblings who modeled Jesus. We went to church every Sunday morning and evening. Several times a week, we were there for extra prayer meetings, choir rehearsals, and fellowships. I gave my life to Christ at the age of 12, and my faith began its growth journey as church pastors, teachers, choir directors, and mentors poured into my young life. God was building my foundation. Life was good.

At age 19, I had a blind date with Doug, the 20-year-old man who would become my husband, my person. We grew up near each other but had never met. We heard about each other through a mutual friend; his from high school, mine from a theatre class at a local junior college. It was a year and a half before we'd meet face to face.

During that time, God was working and preparing both of us for the journey that would become our lifeline. By the end of our first date, we knew we would spend the rest of our lives supporting and loving each other. Through our marriage, since 1988, I've experienced God as Ahavah, learning, through His gentle guidance, His true unwavering and unconditional love.

Our baby boys came along in March, 1991 and December 1993. We had always lived in Texas. However, in 2001, God moved us to Southern California through a job transfer with Doug's employer. While on our house-hunting journey before our move, we visited Venice Beach. As a house-warming gift, we purchased a large print of Michelangelo's *Creation*. In true Texas form, it was so big, it wouldn't fit in the rental car without pushing our seats forward literally into the dashboard, scooting down into the seat and stuffing it over our heads for the hour ride back to the hotel. We still laugh about it to this day! It would hang on our staircase as a reminder of God's fingerprint, and how every moment of our move had fallen into place.

Our faith deepened as we found our home church in Lake Elsinore and made the most amazing lifelong friends. Our hearts were full. In 2004, again through my husband's job, God saw fit to move us—this time to a suburb of Atlanta.

The *Creation* print would move along with us to hang this time, over the fireplace. God's fingerprint had, once again, carved out our place in Loganville, Georgia. Our foundation of faith as a family continued to grow, again, making lifelong friends who would carry us through some of the most difficult moments of our lives.

Back home in Texas, our parents were aging, and in 2012 God blessed us once again. We were transferred back to Texas to be closer to family, and you guessed it, the *Creation* print would hang in this home as well. In every move, every moment, God proved himself faithful in preparing our journey. He became Jehovah Jireh, our God of Provision. He was strengthening our faith for the very steps that we would be taking for the next 10 years.

> For the eyes of the Lord run to and fro throughout the whole earth to prove Himself strong on behalf of those whose hearts are loyal to him.
>
> 2 Chronicles 16:9, NKJV

> Even there Your hand will lead me, Your right hand will take hold of me.
>
> Psalm 139:10, AMP

The events of June, 2012 and forward were some of the longest, hardest, and most difficult moments of our lives. This is when the "fly in my coffee" showed up the most! We left our then 18-year-old and 21-year-old sons in Georgia. As my husband left each day to go to work, I was at home doing my best to navigate the long moments of silence like I had never experienced.

I sank into a place of deep depression that took every breath. Although I continued to read my Bible, sing and smile, work out, and be hopeful of the future—I didn't know how to live without my boys. God had proven Himself faithful over and over, and yet, I needed to know my boys were okay—really okay. As we left them behind to move into our next phase of life, I wasn't able to truly know how they were managing on their own. In all honesty, it broke me. God became Jehovah-Shalom. My peace.

My first born, Austin, was, and still is, a ball of energy. He came into the world completely on the move and has never stopped. He went through some very difficult times through his teenage years, but he trusted the Lord at a young age. God's fingerprint has always been so obvious in his life, leading and directing Austin's every step. He is truly my sunshine!

My second born, Colton, was the happiest baby ever. He was content to play and loved to laugh. He was laid back but had a wicked sense of humor. He also trusted the Lord at a young age, although he continually struggled throughout childhood, his teen years, and into adulthood with anxiety, depression and anger. By the time Doug and I moved back to Texas, Colton had been arrested twice and gone to jail. He was arrested once more in Georgia after the move, and probation became his keeper. He was not allowed to cross the state line.

But, by God's hand (and without the strenuous details), Colton was able to move to Texas. This was a miracle for us, and God's fingerprint was all over it. Austin was able to move back as well. Prayers answered. Our boys were home! God became Jehovah Nissi, my God of Miracles.

In 2013 we moved my parents in with us and we began looking at more permanent living quarters on their behalf. My mom was diagnosed with dementia at 70 years old, and it progressed further to the point that my father became her memory. My father was diagnosed with cancer in 2014 and passed away five weeks later. Mom remained on her own for a few months, with her friends, family, and I checking in daily.

It became clear, after a little while, that she would need 24/7 care. At the time, I was unable to move her in with me, as my youngest son was continually struggling with addiction, leaving our home a very insecure place for someone with dementia. After much prayer and consideration, we found an assisted living facility that would become her home for the next year and a half.

Austin married the love of his life in 2016, and he and his wife, Heather, settled in Georgia. Then, for the first time ever, on Mother's Day, 2017, Colton gave me the most beautiful yellow roses with red tips along with the sweetest card. He was upset that the handwritten note inside made me cry, but I explained that I cried because it was perfect.

Five days later, on May 20, 2017, my world turned upside down and inside out. The "fly in my coffee" was not just a common housefly. This one was a HUGE Texas horsefly that bit and stung worse than any other experience of my life.

It was a Saturday, and my mom and I had gone to Lubbock the day before to attend my cousin's wedding, expecting to return on Sunday. The morning of the 19th, I closed the front door behind me and started to go back into the house to kiss Colton, and tell him I loved him. Instead, I dismissed it and thought, rather than waking him, "I'll see him Sunday."

Early Saturday morning, around 1:15 am, I was awoken by my mom. She was at the side of our bed looking for something. When I asked her what she was looking for, she replied, "Oh… I was looking for you," and she promptly returned to bed beside me, wrapping her arms around me for the next 30 minutes or so. I have to be honest when I say in the moment, I was just trying to sleep and was wishing she would roll over and leave me be.

Then my phone rang. I knew from experience that my phone ringing in the middle of the night was never good news. Expecting to see Colton's name, I quickly picked it up. However, it was a number that I didn't recognize. The woman on the other end stated that she was with Colton at the local hospital in our hometown. I was 300 miles away, so I called my husband immediately and waited for what seemed like eternity to hear something.

A few minutes later, I was reminded of how short life is; my 23-year-old son had taken his last breath—and a part of me along with him. The five-hour drive home was brutal, full of uncontrollable tears, many phone calls, and gut-wrenching conversations. I even pulled over for gas and broke down with the girl at the counter. She prayed with me, and I believe that prayer led me through the rest of my journey home.

I was never so thankful to get back, while at the same time, I came to the rawness of my faith. Did I question God? You bet I did! The God I trust is the God of Miracles and Hope. Where was my miracle and how could I ever hope again?

Over the next few months, I screamed when I could find a moment. I doubled over in pain and thought my heart would surely burst. My head pounded. My mind raced, trying to find some sense of direction. I regretted not going back inside the house that morning to hug my baby boy.

I had been with him for his first breath and through every bump and bruise; I sang to him to calm his fears and hurts. I regretted that I couldn't be there—at least to hold him, when he took his last breath.

So did I really trust God like I had always said I did? I wanted to run and keep running, running, running, further and further away. And then I realized, those arms holding me when I received that call were not my mother's arms, but the arms of the compassionate, loving God, as He was preparing me for my next breath, my next heartbeat, my next question, my next moment—and I ran

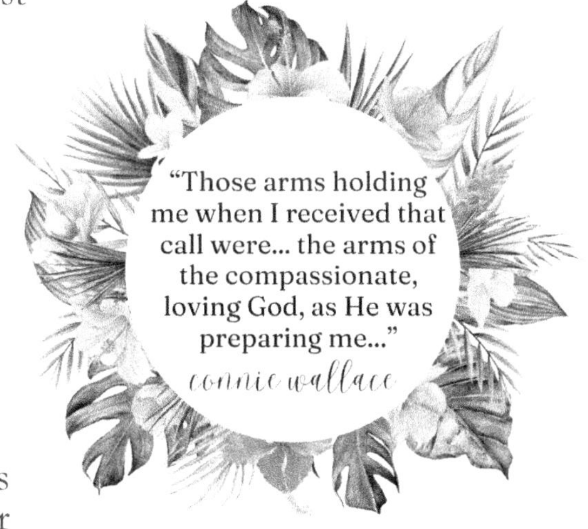

back into His arms of protection and strength. Yes… He is the God of Miracles and Hope!

And He has promised to never leave or forsake you and me. I am standing on this promise, although sometimes it's second by second.

> No one will be able to stand against you all the days of your life. For I will be with you as I was with Moses. I will not fail you or abandon you.
>
> Joshua 1:5, NLT

Never before or since have roses lasted so long. They wilted after about three weeks, and were totally dried up by the fourth. I placed them in a zip-lock bag until I could take them to work and press them. They stayed in the baggie for a week or so, and when I finally got the chance, I started pulling them apart. The pain was unbearable. The tears streamed more and more with the pull of every petal.

I was still questioning God: "Is Colton okay?" "Is Colton with You?" "Why did this have to happen?" "I expected a miracle for him, God."

And then, I came to the single rose that would change my outlook forever! As I pulled the final petals, now dull brown, withered, and completely dried, God revealed the most vibrant, brand-new rosebud with a pinkish-purple center, growing from inside. I immediately knew that Colton was with Him, at peace, and living a new, more complete life beyond my feeble comprehension. Another Miracle!

Over and over, throughout my journey, God has proven Himself faithful and merciful with His gentle fingerprint guiding every moment. The Bible tells us that He orders every step. In my experience, every step we take prepares us for the next.

Colton's passing, as brutal and difficult as it was, allowed my then 79-year-old mom to move in with us for the rest of her days on earth. When she took her journey to heaven in July 2018, God began preparing me for the next season.

Our first granddaughter was born ten days before Mom's passing. We experienced so much joy—yet so much grief all at the same time. A few months later, in March 2019, my in-laws were in need of care. The experience I had with my mom led to becoming a caregiver for them until the passing of my father-in-law in 2020 and mother-in-law in 2022.

It was so clear that God had prepared me for them, and them for me. His fingerprint directed conversations, wound care, hospital stays, medical needs, and provided wisdom for every part of their final days. There is nothing better than being where God has planted you and seeing His hand at work. My mom once asked me after our move to California, "Honey… Aren't you homesick?" and my reply was, "Mom… It's so hard to be homesick when you're right where God wants you."

God directs the steps of the righteous, and while they may stumble, they won't fall because He holds them with His hand, offering reassurance even in failure. God provides support and restoration, a promise of guidance and protection for those who delight in Him.

| Psalm 37:23–24, NIV

God is Adonai, Sovereign over life and death. He is sovereign over every "fly in my coffee." His fingerprint has covered your being and my being since the beginning of creation. When He was creating, He was thinking of us. He knows us so intimately, even better than we know ourselves, and He wants nothing but the best for us. He is bigger than every loss, fear, failure—the list can go on and on.

I have learned that He is always smack-dab in the middle of every moment. Unfortunately, my eyes don't always see Him. Oh, how I long to see Him work at every mountain high, every valley low, every bump in the road, and every twist and turn.

Above all, I know He is faithful and gracious. His love never fails. And I can stand on every promise He has spoken.

It is my prayer for you, wherever you are in your little corner of the world, that God will reveal His presence in every part of your journey. As He lifts your head and sings over you with joy, may you know His heart is always with and for you!

All glory to God for opening this door for me to share my story. Blessings and love to my husband, Doug, for his unwavering and unending support as I've walked through the learning process(es) of putting my words on paper. And to my son, Austin and Daughter-in-law, Heather, thank you for every form of encouragement you have given during this process. Thanks, specifically, for your help with my lack of social media skills! And to my grandbabies, Finley, Stellan, and Remi— you are the joy that propels me forward! Each of you holds my heart and completes my every passion.

Prayer to God

Heavenly Father, The one True God,

I lift my friends, family, acquaintances, and myself to you. May You hold us in the palm of Your hand until the day of redemption. May we find You and trust in You for every breath and direction as we walk through every moment of our lives. May we always see Your hand at work with eyes of faith and a heart of understanding as You are proving Yourself faithful in every circumstance. Thank you, Lord, that You are loving, compassionate, gracious, merciful, powerful and present when we seek You!

In Your Precious, Holy, and Amazing name,

Amen!

deepening your walk

Scripture Verse

Translations

Key Words

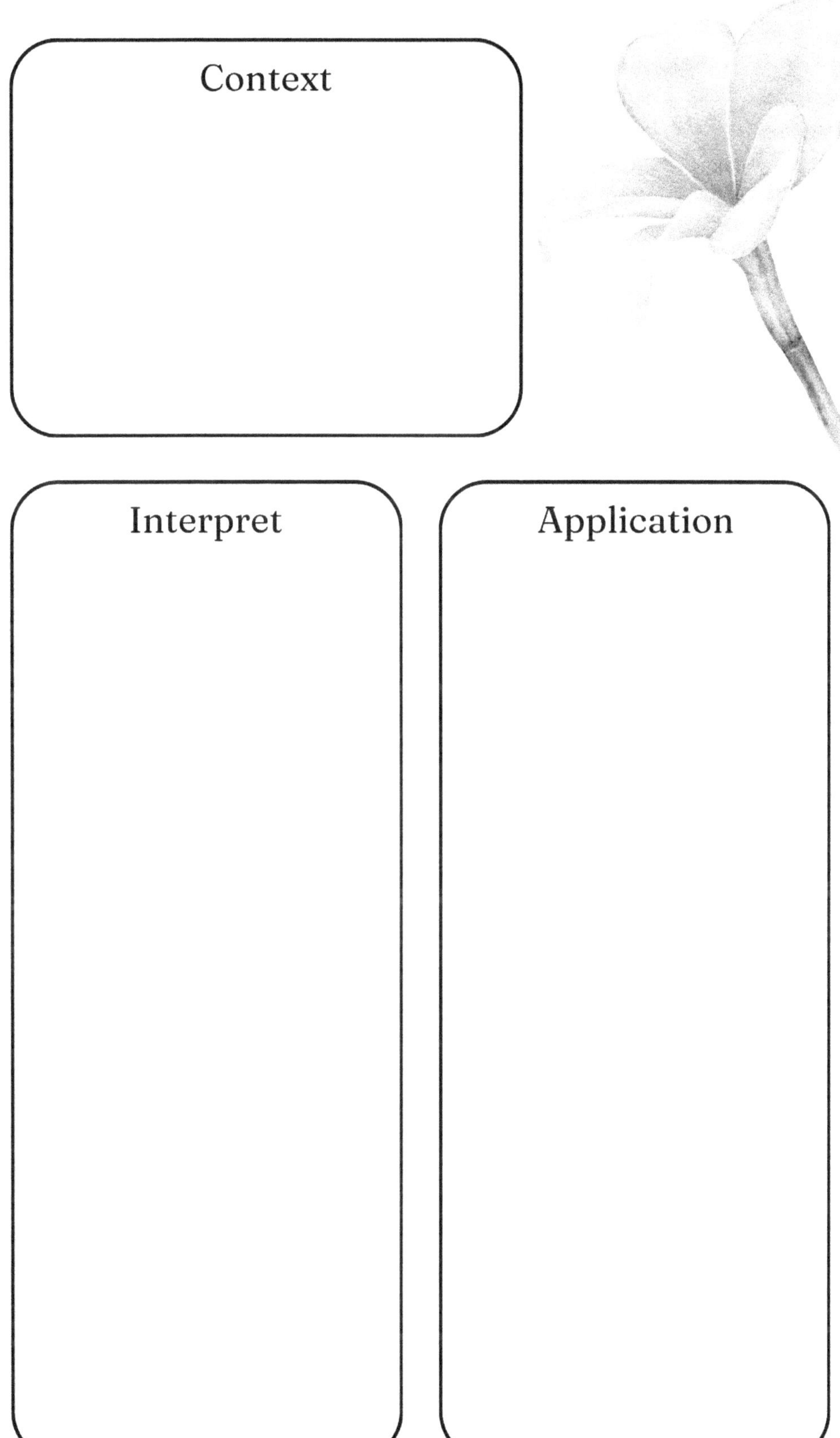

Context

Interpret

Application

strength and courage

Dr. Lynnette Simm

More than likely, you've heard the cliche, *If I can do it, you can do it.*

I'm no different than anyone else. I have had my hardships. I have had my traumas. I have had my challenges—and yet I have had some amazing accomplishments and opportunities and adventures that I would've never had without God.

Growing up, there was no thought in my mind that I would get a college education—let alone get a Doctorate in Education. I have been surprised, delighted, and sometimes frustrated with the blessings that God has given me. I'm hoping that you found this book because you have a delight in the Lord. Or perhaps someone gave you this book to encourage you to seek Jesus as your Lord and Savior.

Allow me to share how Jesus helped me to bravely be me, and turned my pain and my trials into helping others.

What I admire about Joshua is that he was not born into leadership. He was not born to lead—he was called to do it. For those of you who don't know Joshua in the Bible, he was the son of Nun, who was part of one of the twelve tribes of Israel. But most importantly, Joshua was a man who followed Moses. Moses was chosen by God to get the Israelites out of Egypt. He was charged with taking the Israelites to the promised land. But the people were not happy about leaving Egypt and all of its benefits, even though they had been in slavery for many years. Their grumbling made God angry, so the Israelites and Moses, along with Joshua, spent forty years in the wilderness. After Moses passed, God allowed His people into the promised land of what we now know as Israel. Then, God called Joshua to lead the people. Joshua was faithful to Moses for forty years—and he saw the hardship Moses went through trying to lead this group of people. So, while an honor, I'm sure it was quite difficult for Joshua to comprehend the idea that he was now going to have to lead God's people.

In Joshua 1:3, God tells Joshua that every place the sole of his foot treads upon God will give to him. Let's think about every place that our feet have treaded. All of the trials and tribulations, pains and hurts, joys and excitement. All of those places that we have gone through—the Lord is going to bless us.

As we learn from Joshua, it's not going to be easy. Trials are never easy, because if they were, we wouldn't need God—we would do it ourselves.

God goes on to tell Joshua that no man will stand before him for all of Joshua's days, but most importantly, He reminds Joshua that He will never leave or forsake him.

There are a lot of people who come in and out of our lives, but we are still standing. I am still here, writing this for you, and you are still there, wherever you are, reading this. And that is because of God's promise to never leave and never forsake us.

But how do we survive? How do we keep standing and moving forward? How did Joshua do it?

God gave Joshua instructions.

God begins by saying to Joshua in verse 6, "Be strong and of good courage." And again God says in verse 7, "Only be strong and very courageous…" God warns Joshua that the best way for him to stay on his path of leadership is to meditate on the Books of the Law, which were written to help us prosper and succeed.

God then repeats, "Be strong and of good courage. Do not be afraid, or dismay; for the Lord your God is with you wherever you go." Finally, God commands Joshua to tell His people that Joshua is in charge, to create an army of men, and ensure that the women and children will stay back in the promised land while the men go out and conquer the surrounding areas around them. God ends this chapter by saying, "Only be strong and of good courage." The rest of the book of Joshua recounts the journey that Joshua and his army take as they go from battle to battle, conquering the enemy. There's a moment where Joshua goes back to the Lord in the Lord, who reiterates again to be strong and of good courage. God reminds Joshua that He is with him and that He will not forsake him.

The story of Joshua brings my mother to mind.

My mother faced devastating circumstances, yet she got up every day and tried her best. Pregnant at 17, my mother dropped out of high school and married her boyfriend by age 18, creating the stable family she didn't have. With three children, she divorced my biological father by age 21 because he was using drugs and alcohol, physically abusing her, and cheating on her. But my mom tried love again and married my dad, and gained a stepchild. She struggled through living paycheck to paycheck, another alcoholic husband, and years of depression.

Things went from bad to worse for my mother: another broken husband, a stepchild who left because of the physical abuse and chaotic alcoholic behavior, a son running wild and getting into trouble, a sick child with a life altering disease, and a daughter—me—who had been sexually abused for years.

But then, she prayed—and God answered her: "Be strong and courageous." Like Joshua witnessed Moses, I witnessed life with my mother, Louise. Truthfully, I didn't see her strength, nor did I see her pray. What I thought I was witnessing was a weak woman who would rather stay with a man who hurt her and her children, rather than leave and be strong. A huge part of me hated her for this, and I let her know it.

For over fifteen years, my pain and hatred drove me. I thought, *I will show her.* I would be different than her. I wouldn't let my husband control me. I wouldn't quit school. I would be stronger, smarter, and better than her. But instead, I became a passive-aggressive, self-righteous, judging woman. I pretended to the outside world that I had it all together, but really, I kept all the bitterness and anger inside and unleashed it on my husband and children. I would take it out on my mom and dad, my siblings, and other family members. I kept behaving this way until I nearly destroyed my marriage, my girls, and every relationship in my family. But then—I prayed.

Jesus told me to "be strong and courageous." He forgave me and asked me to do something I thought I could never do: forgive my mom, my dad, my biological father, and myself. Jesus wanted me to choose forgiveness and restoration, to choose to walk with HIM and lean on Him, even though I had no idea how or where it would take me.

But He knew. Jesus gave me strength that surpasses all understanding. He gave me the help I needed to heal from my pain, traumas, and finally release my bitterness and hatred. This type of courage is what led me to find therapists, mentors, and groups that I needed to find healing, forgiveness, and release. God deepened my faith in His love, showed me that I was never alone, and allowed me to grow in wisdom of true courage and strength.

He allowed me to see that it would have been easier for my mother to have left my dad and for my dad to have left our family. But they both choose to stay and take responsibility for their actions, to stay and take all the hurt and anger from me, and to stay and keep loving me, even through my hatred and pain. God allowed me to see the kind of strength that allowed them both to quit drinking and to help my father heal and grow into an amazing husband and dad. This type of courage allowed my mom to believe in love and forgiveness. This type of forgiveness allowed my dad to pour into her for their 45 years of marriage.

After God opened my eyes to what He led my mom to survive, heal, and restore, I was in awe of His greatness. I was finally able to let go and forgive. And I allowed Jesus to help me, too—to become strong, courageous, and brave.

This kind of strength and courage is what allowed me, with my family, to restore our relationships and see our Lord and Savior bring our family together in ways that still amaze me. God's grace allowed me to hold my dad's hand and tell him I love him and that Jesus loves him as he left this world. The strength God gave me allowed my mother to pass away quietly in her sleep, knowing her family was

healed and strong, and that the Lord would never leave them or forsake them.

God never left us, even when we didn't see Him in our lives. He gave us what we needed to be strong and courageous.

Being *you* bravely is your offering to the Lord. Sometimes we think strength and courage come from some huge superhero event—but more times than not, strength and courage is simply getting up the next day. Doing the next thing. Making it to work one more day and getting the bills paid. Getting food, clothes, supplies for our children one more day. Taking calls from our children, our loved ones, or our friends in need. Leaning into the Lord and trusting him with everything, even though you have no clue how you're going to get through what you're going through.

That's how I see courage. Courage means the mental or moral strength to venture out, to persevere, to withstand or deal with danger, fear, or difficulty. It's important to understand that it's not about NOT being fearful or NOT feeling overwhelmed and it's not even about NOT feeling incapable or defeated. Because courage isn't a feeling; courage is an action.

Courage is perseverance in the face of adversity. Courage is the mental, emotional, and spiritual strength that comes from God in our time of need.

There is a difference between being brave and being courageous. Bravery is seen as something that is absent of fear, and in contrast, courage doesn't mean that you're not afraid. It means that you do it anyway. However, I believe when we have the Lord, knowing that HE is not going to leave or forsake us, we have both bravery and courage. Bravery because we know that no matter what, God is there, reducing our fear. And for me, sometimes it makes me almost fearless, because I know I can't make a mistake that God won't use.

Whatever trial, pain, or experience, God will use it for my good and for the good of others. But being courageous means knowing that even though I can experience fear, God's plan is greater, bigger, and better than anything I could imagine. And if I just put one foot in front of the other, one day at a time, He will provide. He did that for Joshua, for my parents, Bob and Lousie, and for Madison, my husband, and me. God can do it for you, too.

The most important thing for you to do is to follow God's instruction in scripture. You can grow your bravery, courage, and strength by strengthening your relationship with the Lord. You can learn, grow, and develop new skills for healing. When you expand your emotional strength, your courage increases. Trust me: if I can do it, you can do it too.

How can we become more courageous?

1. Deal with Fear

First, we must acknowledge that we can be fear-filled people. But we must understand fear is usually false. It can merely be an insecurity that is manifesting in fear. Once we acknowledge that that fear is false, we are one step closer to a courageous journey. As we make it a habit to bring our fears before the Lord, we can make it a habit to become braver.

> You are my servant; I have chosen you and have not cast you away. Fear not, for I am with you; Be NOT dismayed for I am your God. I will strengthen you. Yes, I will help you, I will uphold you with MY righteous right hand.
>
> Isaiah 41:9–10, NKJV

2. Declare the Goodness of the Lord

We can learn to lean into the Lord and remind ourselves to talk positively about what God has created. We were created in his image, and we were created perfectly. That doesn't mean we don't make mistakes, but we have His full forgiveness and full grace. And as we are this side of heaven, with every mistake, we get to learn and grow closer to the Lord.

> I will praise YOU, for I am fearfully and wonderfully made; Marvelous are Your works, and that my soul knows very well.
>
> Psalm 139:14, NKJV

3. Trials Grow Us

Learning and growing can be difficult. We must remember that in this life, things will be hard and uncomfortable. We will have to deal with the highest of highs and some of the lowest of lows—and everything in between. It is with every trial and tribulation that we grow stronger.

> My brothers and sisters, count it all joy when you fall into various trials, knowing that the testing of your faith produces patience. But let patience have its perfect work, that you may be perfect and complete, lacking in nothing.
>
> James 1:2–4, NKJV

> And not only that, but we also glory in tribulations, knowing that the tribulation produces perseverance; And perseverance, character and character, hope period now hope does not disappoint, because the love of God has been poured out in our hearts by the Holy Spirit who was given to us.
>
> Romans 5:3–5, NKJV

4. Meditate on His Word

We need to practice meditating on His word and on His promises again and again. This will strengthen us to our core—deep into our souls—so we can battle the things of this world. With prayer and with worship we come into connection with the Lord; to communicate our gratitude, to give him our worries and fears, and to remind ourselves of His love, forgiveness, and grace. What is wonderful about meditating on the Lord is that you can never over-meditate. You can never over-pray, you can never over-worship.

> But His delight is in the Law of the Lord, and in His law he meditates day and night.
>
> Psalm 1:2, NKJV

> Rejoice always, pray without ceasing, in everything give thanks; for this is the will of God in Jesus Christ for you.
>
> 1Thessalonians 5:16–18, NKJV

5. Build Community

Finally, the best way to have courage, the best way to strengthen our bravery, is through community. God created us for community. Community with Him and community with one another.

> And the Lord God said, "It is not good that man should be alone…"
>
> Genesis 2:18, NKJV

> A new commandment I give to you, that you love one another. As I have loved you, that you also love another. By this all will know that you are my disciples, if you have love for one another.
>
> John 13:34–35, NKJV

> And let us consider how to stir up one another to love and (do) good works, not neglecting to meet together, as it is the habit of some, but encouraging one another, and all the more as you see the Day (of the Lord) drawing near.
>
> Hebrews 10:24–25, ESV

> ...from whom the whole body, joined and held together by every joint with which it is equipped, when each part is working properly, makes the body grow so that it builds itself up in love.
>
> Ephesians 4:16, ESV

We can be with the Lord and communicate with Him through scripture, prayer, and worship.

deepening your walk

Scripture Verse

Translations

Key Words

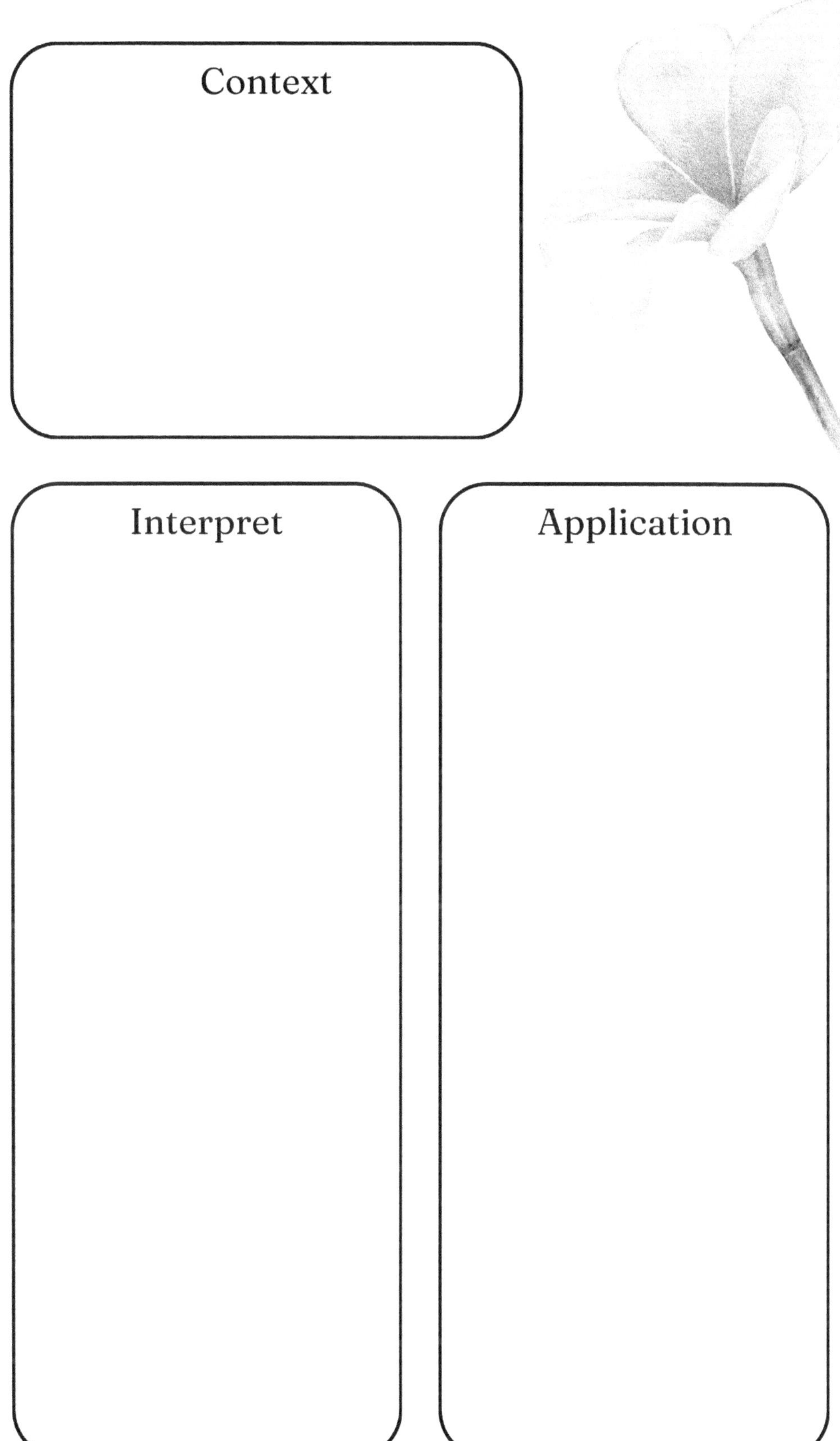
Context
Interpret
Application

STUCK TO SURRENDER

Stuck between here and heaven
There is bliss in a present,
but I dream endlessly of Heaven with you
A warm hug
Euphoric comfort
Rocking us both to sleep
But, for now,
I'm stuck between here and heaven.

In prayer, God said

"Write about Surrender so that I can
heal your heart and mind.
Let God in to heal you. He is safe
You don't have to be afraid anymore."

God said to use my trauma and pain
to show others there is freedom from fear with Him.
You must surrender to be healed.

My prayer for the woman living in fear:
Sister, there is safety in your surrender to God.
Let him comfort and heal you.

I declare that nothing will be impossible with God
Luke 1:37

I declare that Jesus, anxiety and depression
will not dominate my heart.
I declare that my joy comes from Jesus!
I declare that God is a mighty healer!

—Autumn Price

Lord, I hate to wait!

Elise Anthony

I've seen You move, You move the mountains
And I believe I'll see You do it again
You made a way, where there was no way
And I believe I'll see You do it again

— "Do It Again" by Elevation Worship

"And now, O Lord, for what do I wait? My hope is in you.

Psalm 39:7, ESV

The lights were down; the room was full. The piano began slowly as the praise team eased into a popular Elevation Worship song.

> Walking around these walls
> I thought by now would fall…

Standing alone in the dark, something inside me crumbled. Tears started falling as I cried.

Being single was my Jericho. My heart desperately longed to be loved.

> Waiting for change to come
> Knowing the battle's won

I'd been divorced for more than 10 years. I've been a Christ follower for decades. In that moment though, the battle sure didn't feel "won." Not even close. I felt hopeless as I stood there, surrounded by couples. Mercifully, someone put their arm around me and held on.

I felt guilty mourning my singleness while so many others are truly suffering heartbreak, loss, tragedy. I have a great life and loving family and friends. My testimony has always focused on how God has been so very good to me.

Yet … *I grieved.* My smile couldn't entirely hide the loneliness that followed me everywhere: Parties, holidays, and milestones continued to pass me by.

As the song proceeded, I surrendered my grief to the Lord. This time, I truly heard one of the lyrics:

> You've never failed me yet.

The truth hit; God has never failed me. Not even once. The Holy Spirit reminded me of His faithfulness and a lifetime of victory, protection, and provision. I leaned deeply into my faith. I continued attending church and serving.

Years later, I made peace with my singleness. There's something about building a new home and designing it brick by brick without a spouse that cements the reality of depending solely on the Lord—and no one else.

When I finally met my forever person, the wait finally made sense. In God's perfect timing, we both had experienced trials that built patience and endurance that would be instrumental in our future relationship's success. We were both ready for a spiritually-anchored marriage. Hallelujah!

That 17-year journey of waiting taught me to trust God's timing and put my faith in Him. Yet, may I confess something?

I trust God, *but Lord, I hate to wait!*

Each of us will face at least one monumental season of waiting within our lifetime, perhaps more. Walking through the uncertainty and timing of hardship, struggles, and even loneliness have the potential to derail even mature Christians into a crisis of faith.

Decades of trial and error have taught me to be discerning of well-intentioned advice and instead look to the infallible Word of God for my joy.

Fortunately for us late bloomers, the Bible is full of God's beloved children facing epic uncertainty and an ambiguous timeline at best.

- When Isaiah prophesied about Immanuel in Isaiah 7:14, his own son was born less than two years later. Jesus was born about 600 to 700 years afterward.

- David had to wait 15 years between being anointed as king and taking rule after Saul's death.

- Scholars believe it took Noah 50 to 100 years to build the ark.

The Unscheduled Sabbatical

When the next major crisis hit a year and a half after being married, I knew enough to start praying and studying.

God called me into writing at age 17. In the following years, He confirmed it again and again as my career flourished in improbable circumstances. His blessing supported and protected my family. I waited to launch a writing ministry until I felt His timing.

My spirit began stirring several years ago to start writing for the Lord in earnest. I took a few baby steps with an infrequent blog while juggling the needs of a busy career and household. The book? About exploring God's calling for one's life.

Ten days before my 51st birthday, crisis came calling again.

I was laid off by a video call.

The office was eerily empty as I exited corporate life with a half-empty backpack and a few personal possessions.

I didn't know it yet, but my unscheduled sabbatical had begun.

All the obstacles to writing for the Lord fell away.

Weeks earlier, I attended *Surrender*, a women's group led by Yolanda, one of my favorite mentors. We met for seven Sundays, exploring spiritual growth and empowerment. I won a door prize, a pretty sign with the following scripture:

> The Lord will fight for you; you need only to be still.
>
> Exodus 14:14, NIV

My own Bible study class had just begun a two-year study of the book of Exodus. I often notice patterns and repetitions of words; was the Lord trying to tell me something?

Verse by verse, I read the book of Exodus with a fresh perspective, realizing God's chosen people lived—and waited—through centuries of uncertainty. Yet, He rescued them, even when they continually sinned against Him.

Several weeks after my corporate exodus, I decided to treat my unexpected time off like a sabbatical. I would write like I see in the movies, cozily tucked away in a cabin in the woods, no TV nor internet, warm cup of coffee in hand. I earmarked two months for book writing, and then I would return to the land of the gainfully employed.

(If you have written a book before, you are probably laughing hard or at least nodding in agreement with good intentions and the bliss of not knowing how hard it is to undertake such a project.)

Distractions and distress set in.

Days morphed into weeks, and somehow spring became the end of the year. I was fully engulfed in an identity crisis unlike anything I'd ever encountered. The sheer stress of receiving rejection after rejection during a brutal job market squashed my confidence and I struggled with conflicting feelings and emotions about feeling worthy.

No one tells you how you'll grieve the loss of coworkers you spend more time with than most family members or friends.

No one mentions how the loss of routine unsettles your life.

And no one can predict the length of a season such as this.

Here I was, writing a book about how to explore God's calling for your life, and I couldn't seem to get the words to flow or find the discipline and confidence to continue my own calling. Even getting a job as a writer or editor proved to be impossible as doors continued to close one by one.

Meanwhile, as I struggled to complete chapters about identity, strongholds, and pursuing a calling, I realized I was living out my own book, chapter by chapter.

Character defects? Check.

Imposter Syndrome? Check.

Strongholds? Yep.

Each chapter had its own challenges as my crisis unfolded over worries about finances, self-worth, and purpose.

I realized that, at some point in my life, I allowed my career to become an idol; I was putting more faith in it than the One who created me. No wonder I was on unsteady ground.

Depression upheaved my days and nights. I slept too much and not enough; I regained weight I had lost two years prior. Some days were productive, others not so much. Even though I was home all day, my house was messier and more cluttered than ever.

Between the pages, however, God was preparing me.

Pruning & Preparing

The more I researched for my book, the more I delved into God's Word. If I am to be a writer for the Lord, His calling for me would require me going much, much deeper in His Word. Maybe you can relate.

Indeed, there is a verse for this:

> Trust in the Lord with all your heart, and do not lean on your own understanding.
>
> Proverbs 3:5, ESV

Leaning on my own understanding was creating a secondary crisis of confidence.

A chapter I wrote about character defects and fruit of the spirit convicted me; I began to scrutinize what's going right in my life, and where changes need to be made. The Lord remained close to me as I sought Him and asked Him what I should do next.

It didn't take long to realize that if I want spiritual growth at a kingdom level, Jesus is the vine, and my branches need pruning. I just had to be open to the process.

> May integrity and uprightness preserve me, for I wait for you.
>
> Psalm 25:2, ESV

One by one, unhealthy habits, character defects, and stumbling blocks became readily apparent. Honestly, it was overwhelming.

Am I willing to start pruning? Am I open to what God is preparing me for? Will I embrace the opportunity to walk closer with the Lord than ever before?

Yes, God.

The difference between this season and prior seasons is that the spirit of peace was upon me because I've seen what the Lord has done in my life. And like the Elevation Worship song says:

> I've seen You move, You move the mountains
> And I believe I'll see You do it again
> You made a way, where there was no way
> And I believe I'll see You do it again
>
> — "Do It Again" by Elevation Worship

We're Never Alone

Another difference stood out during this season: I realized I'm powerless to do all of this by myself.

More and more, I slowly understood what scripture meant by the body of a church behaving as one, each person serving a valuable purpose.

He promises we don't endure difficulty alone, and He exceedingly delivered comfort and company from Godly friends and even strangers.

It's no accident that I belong to a "hospital church," where people can let go of their secrets and allow healing to begin. God steered me there when I met my future husband, and I married into a church family who blessed me beyond measure.

Friends became "framily" as life got harder. These are the people who show up even when you don't know what to ask for. I'm talking about "safe people" you can trust to teach, comfort, encourage, and guide you in God's trust. In turn, I also am there for my church tribe, too.

The Lord also led me to do something the old me would never have done: My newfound time allowed me to try new things, travel, and take classes and join small groups of interest at my church.

Within a year and a half, I attended the equivalent of 10 semesters of small groups and classes, learning to:

- Sustain a healthy marriage and family
- Live a life of pure hope
- Experience God abundantly

I served and volunteered in meaningful ways. My schedule was no longer an excuse for doing the bare minimum. And when you are serving the Lord in a state of surrender, open to whatever God wants you to do and learn, blessings big and small start flowing.

- It's the high five from a preteen who just learned how to introduce himself and how to disagree well during an inner-city summer camp.
- It's sharing a phone screen in part Farsi, part English for a prayer request for newcomers to the U.S.
- It's the ability to sit with a friend at the hospital and not be rushed.

Week over week, I kept experiencing "divine appointments," those unexpected moments, meetings, and conversations where it's certain that the Holy Spirit connected me to someone who had something special to share with me, or vice versa.

Scriptures, testimonies, prayers—each time I stood near the church doorway, someone crossed my path with a little tidbit that I needed for my book. My husband and I once visited another church to attend a friend's wedding afterward, and the message that morning became a touchstone to a chapter I'd struggled to write. Would it surprise you to know we had arrived early and caught the wrong service? And that sermon wasn't repeated in the second service.

These divine moments fueled my faith, even as I struggled with fear and depression. God's Word reminded me of His promises, and His sovereignty over all circumstances and situations.

These reassurances brought peace, contentment, and gratitude as I realized what I have in Christ is absolutely eternal no matter what.

I had more time than ever to spend with my family. Mercy and grace showered me with encouragement at just the right moments. Just a few weeks after I was laid off, my Dad accepted Christ as His Savior, and I stood with him in the lake on a perfect day in May as he was baptized with his new church family watching.

Other moments abounded in absolute joy, too. A mother-son trip to NYC. A little getaway with friends to the Texas Hill Country, where I discovered that I really could hike up Enchanted Rock.

The same friend who told me not to look back is the same one who shouted, "Look how far you've come!" as I hit the halfway spot. And the vista was breathtaking.

As life got real, the conversations got deep in my small groups at church. Finally, I had to confront several uncomfortable truths about myself, one of them being that I have a bona fide food addiction.

Something Has To Break

Addiction is a stigmatizing word in our society. Often, it's hidden away with a hope that no one discovers an inward turmoil that others don't seem to struggle with.

However, discussing addiction in a safe setting puts light on the darkness. Doing life the way I'd been going about it wasn't working. A 12-step group gave me the clarity I needed.

I was broken. My identity as I knew it was broken. Until I addressed it, I couldn't move forward into my calling and into healthy living.

A mentor told me to start looking at my triggers and journal about it. It was through that process that the layers fell away—and I could finally understand.

I'd been living in the spirit of rejection. Every time I felt rejected, consciously or not, I sought comfort. A candy bar became three. A little retail therapy. Whatever gave me the dopamine to feel better.

But, I didn't have to stay that way.

I'm guilty of trying to pray away my character defects and temptations and not do anything else. My mentor writes of a similar struggle: "Lord, just take them away!" she prayed. One day, I recognized myself in her writing.

Once again, the Bible provides insight and wisdom of how to respond. Paul had a "thorn in his flesh," which scholars have debated as a reference to chronic pain or a devastating temptation he fought with. Jesus healed Paul before, so why wasn't Paul healed again?

> But he said to me, "My grace is sufficient for you, for my power is made perfect in weakness." Therefore I will boast all the more gladly of my weaknesses, so that the power of Christ may rest upon me.
>
> 2 Corinthians 12:9, ESV

Ah, the good ol' "count it all joy" reference strikes once again.

There's a scripture that has always unsettled me and for most of my life, I simply could not understand it. I don't believe it's a coincidence that this verse came up in another Sunday sermon:

> Count it all joy, my brothers, when you meet trials of various kinds…
>
> James 1:2, ESV

Admittedly, hearing this verse again wasn't music to my ears. I don't enjoy trials of any kind! I hate to wait, remember? My gut is almost always in panic mode of waiting for the other shoe to drop. I'm not gonna be shouting for joy whenever misfortune hits.

But, I can't just take a verse out of context and assign my own interpretation.

So, back to James 1:

> …for you know that the testing of your faith produces steadfastness. And let steadfastness have its full effect, that you may be perfect and complete, lacking in nothing.
>
> James 1: 3–4, ESV

I meditated on an uncomfortable adage that our pastor often says: *Praying doesn't change God's will, but it does change mine.*

Knowing this has changed my prayer life. Every Sunday, the sermons seemed tailored toward my private prayers. Eventually, truth streamed into my rocky little heart.

When I remove my own expectations of what an answered prayer looks like, God shows up and He shows out.

Joy is not my circumstances. It's a deep-rooted contentment that isn't swayed by temporary matters. Much like love, *joy is a choice.*

Joy CAN co-exist with suffering.

Friends, if you have experienced steadfastness before, you know it's a blessing to be in this state of, shall we say, joy?

The peace I've been experiencing during this season of uncertainty is joyful. It comes from knowing that the Lord is faithful. He's never failed me yet.

Restoration Underway

Joy has a very special presence in our home. Born two days after Christmas, my Grandpa lovingly named my mother Joy. Holiday ornaments, signs, shirts, and all kinds of trinkets that declare JOY are everywhere in our home, but more importantly, my Mom resides here and is a constant reminder of God's love. She is an encourager and my first best friend.

It's our prayer that when people enter the threshold of our home, they experience the peace and joy we have, no matter our circumstances. I have lived in big houses, small apartments, and ones on wheels in a trailer park. I have sacrificed for a dwelling in a good school district and I'm all too guilty of coveting a home that looks like it belongs in a magazine.

Truly, though, a home filled with love is more important than a fashionable ZIP code—and that is a humbling takeaway I won't forget, no matter where we live.

When unemployment benefits ran out and our savings dwindled, financial stewardship became another character issue to confront. As we economized and cut back, a budgeting app helped me be 100% transparent with my spouse. And I am learning to not fill up the empty spaces in my self-worth with things or food.

Friends, it's easy to panic over money—after all, the mortgage isn't going to pay itself. And I am still working on my spending habits in an "essentials-only" economy. But, this time, things are different from other crises I've faced in the past. Tomorrow's financial well-being on this earth is not guaranteed. But I am rich indeed! As a child of the King, but I am inheriting an eternal future with my Creator.

Right now, I don't know how my chapter of waiting ends—and that is simultaneously terrifying and thrilling. There are more questions than answers, but I'm learning to lean on the Lord daily. Every day is a new opportunity to experience God and do the heart work to become more like Jesus.

All good things are possible through Him!

Here is what I do know: waiting builds endurance and prepares us for our next season. If we surrender our hearts and lives to the Lord, He allows us to bear fruit, even in what seems like a barren season. He is always fighting for us and making a way forward.

I marvel at the good works He is doing in my

life. He continues to extend grace and help as I work on character defects, all the while teaching me what I will need for my next season.

Small but mighty changes are happening. I'm a work in progress, and I'm learning that good things take time.

I am not a morning person, but I wake up with a desire to pray and study God's Word. No matter how my schedule changes in the future, time with God is a priority worth choosing. I've created better sleep habits so I have ample time to wake up early, sip coffee, and spend this much-needed time with the Father.

Worship music on, worldly music off. This may not be for everyone, but I need a constant flow of God's truth and encouragement.

As I wrestle with the temptation to dwell on social media, secular music, or any other distraction that's not meant for me, I'm reminded of this verse:

> Keep your heart with all vigilance, for from it flow the springs of life.
>
> Proverbs 4:23, ESV

Prayer journaling is a must, as a writer and as a daughter of the King. I start small, with a daily verse, and listen to commentary on my YouVersion app. I write down the verse and my learnings and meditate in prayer. I add daily prayers and praises, too.

His ways are not our ways, and His timeline isn't the same as our timeline. When I journal consistently, I see His answers to prayers that I'd had for days, weeks—years, even. When my courage fails, He renews me:

> Wait for the Lord; be strong, and let your heart take courage;
> wait for the Lord!
>
> Psalm 27:14, ESV

I'm a cheerful giver who felt discouraged that my lack of income is holding back giving more tangibly to church. As I journaled my prayer, a few days later, an unexpected blessing allowed us to provide something the church needed, at no cost to us, in a way that only God could provide. See, God doesn't just show up; He shows OUT.

Joy is something to meditate upon daily, as I remember and celebrate the finished work of Christ. As God rebuilds me, I am reminded:

> I will restore to you the years that the locust has eaten.
>
> Joel 2:25, ESV

My informal prayer journal is now a book of notes and praises and tangible reminders of God's beautiful work in my messy life.

"God, thank you for the gift of time you have blessed me with to study, learn, write and grow," I wrote one Tuesday morning. "Thank you for the gift of time with friends, family, and church. These relationships and learnings are precious and life-giving."

I am not the same, having walked through this particular season of waiting. But I am renewed and refreshed, ready to follow Him in my next steps and soar.

Reflection

Journal about a situation or unanswered question you are waiting on God to answer. Be real, not religious and pour out your pain, fear, or other feelings.

> The Lord is good to those who wait for him, to the soul who seeks him.
>
> Lamentations 3:25, ESV

What passages from the Bible align with my circumstances? Am I suffering because of the consequences I created? If so, what is my next right step? How will I deal with a prolonged wait?

Prayer to God

Lord,

In the unknown, you are my only known salvation.

As Psalm 39:7 says, my hope is in you.

I don't know what my future holds. I don't even know how today will end. But I do know You are my future.

Lord, please fill me with hope and courage. Please work within me and infuse me with patience and spiritual wisdom to discern what is good and pleasing to you. I want your will, not mine.

Please make my paths straight and reveal your next right step.

Holy Spirit, please counsel and comfort me. Enrich me with joy and gladness over things eternal.

Father God, please take care of my earthly needs and do a good work within me. May your glory shine forever and your love shine in my eyes and in my actions.

You loved me first and I love you more and more daily.

Amen.

> But they who wait for the Lord shall renew their strength; they shall mount up with wings like eagles; they shall run and not be weary; they shall walk and not faint.
>
> Isaiah 40:31, ESV

Dedicated to all those who wait on the Lord. Thank you to my loving friends, family and "framily." Austin, your story is just beginning; being your mommy brought me close to the Lord in prayer daily and you are my legacy. Mom, every day of my life you've encouraged me to dream big and do it; you truly are Joy in my life. Dad, your testimony and salvation fills me with extreme hope. And darling Scott, you were worth the wait.

> Commit your work to the Lord, and your plans will be established.
>
> Proverbs 16:3, ESV

deepening your walk

Scripture Verse

Translations

Key Words

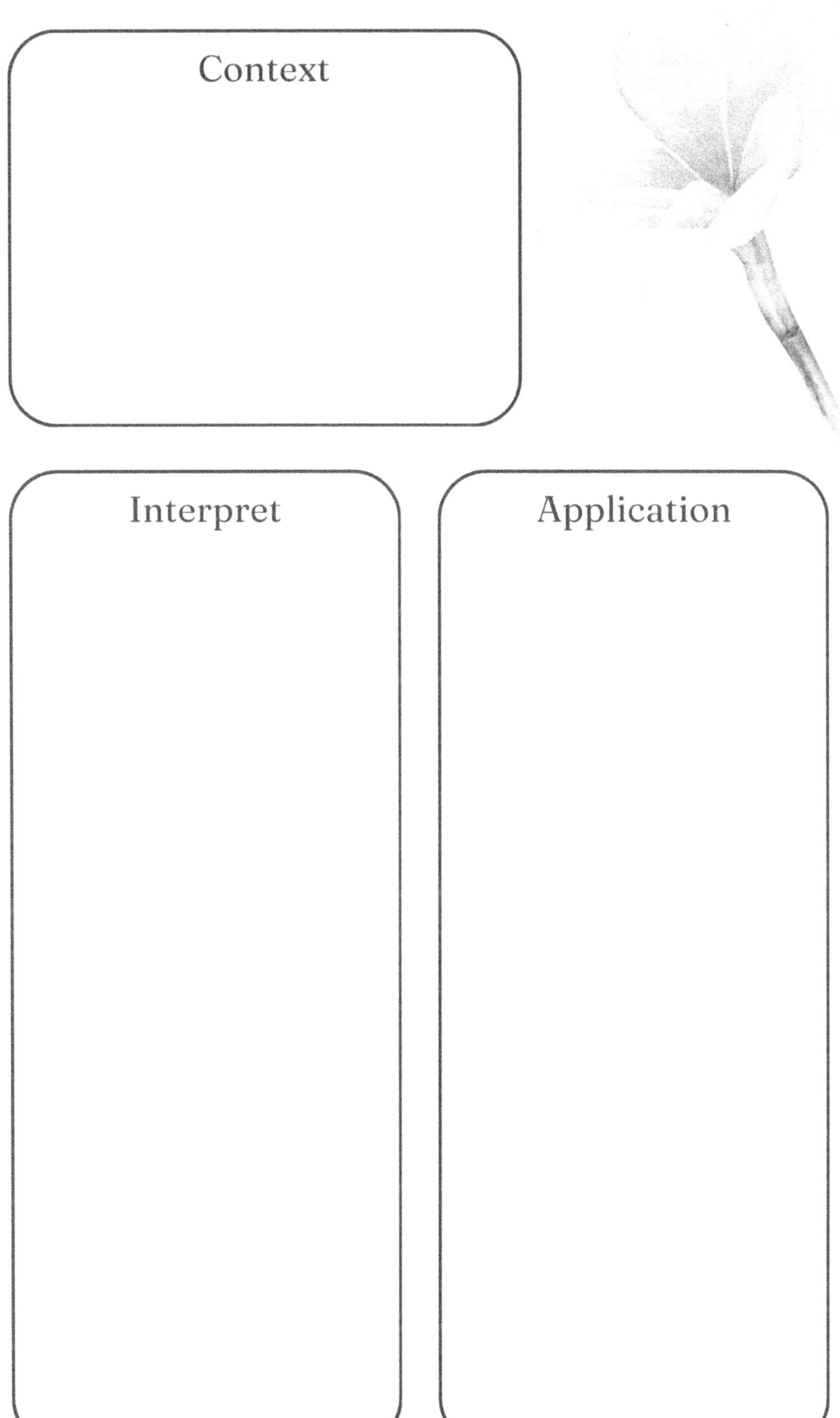

Context

Interpret

Application

is it a tomb or a womb?

Dorothea Shields

When has anything in life ever gone the way you expected or planned?

I can't think of a time when my well laid plans rolled out exactly as I had imagined.

Nor can I think of a time when I asked God to answer a prayer in a specific way, from my "perfect" understanding of the situation, that He said, "Okay, here's your solution. Well played."

It's never happened. I don't have perfect understanding, and in hindsight, His way has always been better, although not without delays, detours, missed turns, and bumps in the road.

But for some reason, I still have this grand idea that if I could crack the code on God's purpose and will for my life, all my problems would be solved. I think that if I knew exactly what God wanted me to do, if I could get a detailed revelation of it, I could go do it, and it would be a simple process of going from point A to point B, and there would be no delays, roadblocks, or hardships along the way.

God doesn't work that way. He never has, and He never will. There's not one single example in the Bible of God working that way. God's way is to take us from point A to point Z with a stop at every point along the way, but not necessarily in the order or direction any of us would anticipate or plan for ourselves.

If I'm being honest, there are times in God's plan when the delays, detours, and bumps feel more like the end of the road, a dead-end, or a tomb than an adventurous journey to a magical fulfillment of my purpose or solution to my problems.

Let's consider the Biblical account of Joseph as an example.

Because of his dreams, he had a clear picture of his future. He was 17 and his dad's favorite, and it seems from the text in Genesis 37 indicates that he was at least a little prideful. His future involved his family bowing down to his greatness. It seemed he had an ideal scenario because God's will was clear and favor was flowing into his life. What could go wrong?

But Joseph's life took several unexpected turns. He was nearly murdered by his brothers and instead sold into slavery, he was falsely accused by his boss' wife, unjustly imprisoned for at least ten years, and forgotten for two of those years. I can't help but wonder if Joseph questioned God and gave up on figuring out what those dreams meant much less believing they would ever come to pass. Who could comprehend that with all the detours and delays if any of those dreams could come to pass? The circumstances of his life were impossible, and I imagine Joseph felt he was living in a dark tomb.

Knowing God's will doesn't insulate us from difficult life circumstances, and Joseph was intimately acquainted with that fact.

So what is it about Joseph's life that we should see in our lives?

It's when we take a bird's eye view of the entirety of Joseph's life, that we see purpose in Joseph's suffering. What seemed like a lifeless, dead-end, and dark tomb was the place of formation, purpose, and destiny.

Joseph wasn't in a tomb but a womb where the Lord was working on Joseph, and at the appointed time, he would be birthed into the manifestation of his destiny.

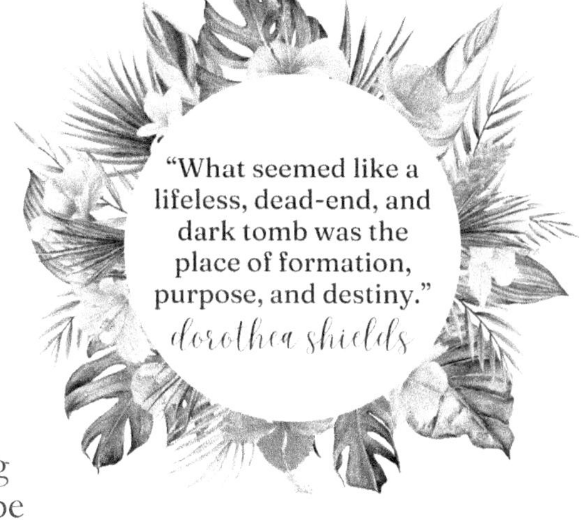

What have you been through? How have you suffered? Did it feel dark and hopeless while you were going through it? And maybe even now, you feel broken and unredeemable.

I'm here to tell you that there is nothing that God can't use, redeem, or turn around. What seems too far gone to you and me is a perfect starting point for our redeeming God.

The beginnings of my life were broken and fractured.

I lost two dads by the time I was six years old: one to divorce and the other to an unexpected death. When I was eight, my mom and I moved across the country from beautiful and mountainous West Virginia to open and barren Texas. The change of scenery was significant because even at eight years old, I felt the loss of natural beauty, as well as the loss of near daily time with my grandparents, my pet Siamese cats (Peppermint and Chocolate Drop), and best friends I'd grown up with to that point. All that was familiar and stable was drastically changed.

From the middle of third grade to when I started high school, I went to a different school every year. I was always the new kid. Whenever I got attached, I was ripped away, or what I loved was ripped away. My subconscious mind determined that to keep me safe from all the instability and loss that it would emotionally detach me from people. Naturally, I still loved my mom and I did have friends, but the depth that I was able to attach was shallow. And I could easily lose close friends and not feel sad.

The issue with emotional detachment is it does keep you emotionally safe to a point, but as nothing bad can pass through nothing good can come in or out. I felt that I had a concrete cap sitting on top of the well spring of my heart. I wanted to feel deep love and give it too, but there was something blocking the flow.

In my young adult years, I became promiscuous, looking for the elusive love, acceptance, and belonging. I hoped to find it all in partying, relationships, and finding my own way in the world. Although I was mostly raised in church and had a relationship with God, I decided when I went to college that I wasn't taking God with me.

I made lots of unhealthy decisions and choices in those years and hurt many people.

I ended up living with my parents and began attending church again. God's kindness led me to repentance, and from that moment, He began healing the broken places and bringing restoration to my life.

What I've learned is that God uses everything.

When I first surrendered my heart to the Lord after having intentionally turned my back on Him, I thought I'd gone too far and that He couldn't use me. I was ok with that because I was just grateful to be back in a relationship with Him. I accepted my fate.

The Lord brought a husband into my life, and I was able to believe that he loved me. Before, I wanted to be loved, but felt rejected and pushed people away because I didn't believe I was loveable. Plus, I believed the lie from my childhood that when I love people, they leave, or the relationship doesn't last. But David was different. It was God's love toward me that flowed through David, and I was able to truly receive the love. It was a miracle and a first step toward healing.

I became a good wife and Christian. We had children and life was in a good place. But no matter how I tried, I couldn't overcome the sense that I was emotionally handicapped.

I learned faith declarations and spoke them over all my negative feelings. But still, nothing inside was changing. I finally began seeing a Christian counselor who told me something that would forever change my life.

I didn't realize it at the time, but the emotional detachment I experienced was my brain's way of protecting me. I understand more about trauma responses nowadays, but I had no clue back then. The trauma was the overwhelming pain and grief from loss and frequent uprooting and instability. My grown-up self was trying desperately to overcome the pain my little girl self experienced and didn't know how to process.

What my counselor told me was that pain cannot be overcome. Pain must be healed.

She showed me a simple but powerful process for receiving healing. Just making faith declarations without actually addressing the underlying issues was keeping me stuck and unable to actually change.

When I began walking through the steps, I quickly experienced a great deal of healing and freedom. The key was being willing to do the steps and take responsibility. Some parts of it are difficult as you must confront your past with courage and humility. The process is effective because it's based on God's word and it's His will to heal you.

The first step is that you must be willing to forgive. Forgiveness is not a feeling, but it's a decision and an act of your will. Forgiving someone, including yourself, is not optional for the believer, and forgiving doesn't mean you're excusing the actions of someone else. You're simply putting the wrong of it into God's hands and letting Him handle it. Sometimes, the hardest person to forgive is yourself. We have all kinds of excuses for holding ourself in unforgiveness, like I knew better, I hurt so many people, I can never do anything right, etc.

When someone is unwilling to forgive, the hard truth is that they are keeping the door to the tormentor wide open. Read Matthew 18:21-35. You must be willing to forgive so you can be released from the torment that unforgiveness brings into your life. When you're willing to make the decision to forgive, you just do it and God will give you grace to walk it out.

The next step is to recognize and take responsibility for the lies you've believed through the years and as a result of the pain that's entered your life. Pain isn't a sin and isn't wrong, but the lies we believe while we're in pain result in sinful behavior. The enemy comes to us with lies when we are vulnerable and in pain from trauma, loss, and grief. It's a sinister plan, and it works because our emotions and situations confirm that the lie must be true. The lies feel true, so we believe them hook, line, and sinker.

I believed the lie that when I love someone they will leave. That led me to reject people and their love, and it led me into destructive and negative patterns of behavior in my search for acceptance, belonging, and purpose.

When I recognized the lie and took responsibility for it, I was then able to go to the next step which is to repent from believing the lie and for the sin I committed as a result of the lie. In this step you're only repenting for the sin you committed, not for anyone else's sin.

Once you have forgiven, recognized and taken responsibility, and repented, you're now ready to renounce the lie and replace it with truth. You must come out of agreement with the lie! And you must use scripture to replace the lie with truth. Whenever your mind wants to go down the well worth pathway in your mind to that old lie, you must put up a barrier and send your mind down a new pathway to the truth. That process is called taking your thoughts captive (2 Corinthians 10:3–5).

Finally, rejoice.

The healing and freedom I experienced from going through this simple process lifted the heaviness in my soul and I began to experience a flow and an expansion of deep and abiding love in my heart. That expansion has continued. I now feel things more deeply, even pain, although through time and intentionality, I'm able to process pain in a healthier way. I believe God desires that for you as well.

The interesting thing I came to realize is that all those years ago God didn't want to set me on a shelf. He wasn't satisfied with my mere return to Him. He wanted to take the brokenness, heal my heart, and form me for the fullness of my purpose and destiny.

Just as God needed to work in Joseph's heart before He could allow him to step into the fullness of his destiny, God is taking you and I through the same process, and has given us Joseph's story to encourage us to continue even when things feel hopeless.

God has a vision for your life just as he had a vision for Joseph's life as well. The darkness of what seemed like a tomb was really a womb where God was developing, shaping, and forming Joseph into the person who could handle his own destiny. With the same care that God tended to Joseph's forming, He is tending to yours.

Your past is of no negative consequence to God. It isn't anything that is insurmountable to Him. There is nothing in your past that could disqualify you from serving God and walking in the fullness of His plans and purposes for you. Ephesians 2:10 says, "For we are His workmanship, created in Christ Jesus for good works, which God prepared beforehand that we should walk in them." He has already made plans for your life, and He wants to get you there. He uses the darkness, the seemingly dead-end tomb like circumstances to actually develop you and grow you into the complete and mature person you need to be to walk in every detail of His plan for your life.

My past is now my testimony that tells of God's power to deliver, heal, restore, and fill with purpose. But I've had to go through the womb of life's hardships to get to this place. I've had to let God heal me so I could grow, mature, and give and receive love.

While your specific circumstances differ from mine, you've been in the womb of life's hardships too. And God is using all those things to give you a testimony of His power and grace.

The tomb and the womb are similar in that they are dark places. The enemy wants us to believe that we're in a tomb where there's hopelessness, despair, and death, but God uses the dark place to remove the junk, fill with His love, give us vision, form us into Jesus' image, and then birth us into our purpose.

There is no death or hopelessness in the God we serve. His nature and kingdom is to go from glory to glory and of the increase of His government there is no end.

I wonder what emotions and ups and downs Joseph went through. You and I can only imagine what we would think and feel if it were us in his situation. I think I would feel frustrated and discouraged because I didn't understand what God was doing. The problem is our expectation, we assume that because we know God's will the road will be easy, and we're shocked when it isn't. I think in Joseph's place I would've felt hopeless and I would've despaired. I can see how easily he could've given up.

In our lives, we so often feel delayed and behind when things slow us down or even when we hit roadblocks. We think we're letting God down and that we'll never accomplish our purpose. It's easy to feel like we're in that tomb with no escape or future in sight. But the womb mentality keeps us focused on God's character, faithfulness, and truth which becomes an anchor for our soul helping us to see that Joseph wasn't really delayed or behind in his destiny, he was actually right on time.

Just as God knew the process and timeline for Joseph's life and was able to form him in the womb of adversity,

God is doing the same for you. God knows your timeline. He knows where you need to be and when you need to be there. If you're actively seeking God, trusting Him, and wanting to walk in His will for your life, you can lean into Joseph's story, have abiding faith and joy that God is using your past for His glory, healing your heart, and forming you to birth you into your purpose and eternal destiny.

deepening your walk

Scripture Verse

Translations

Key Words

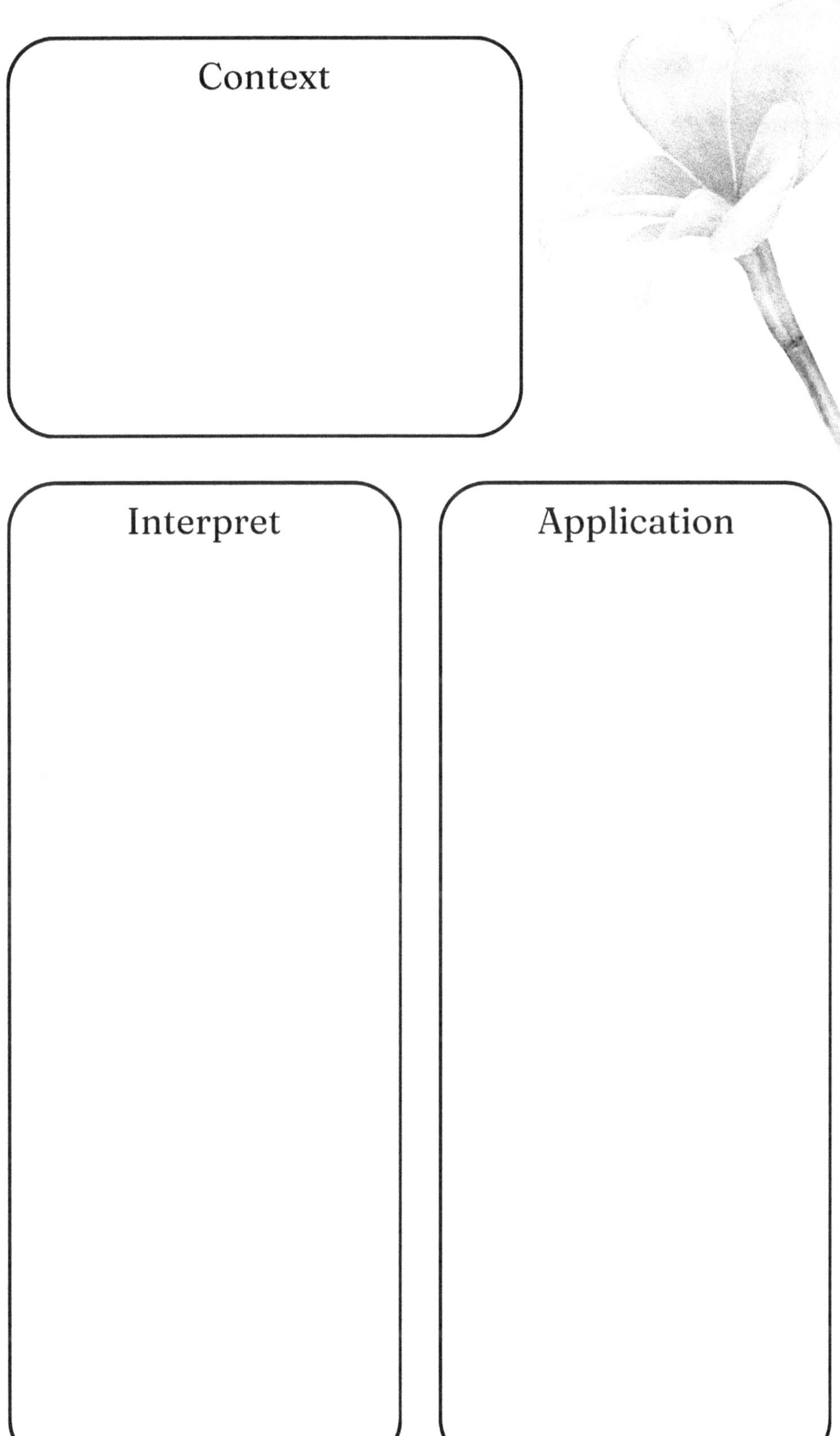

Context

Interpret

Application

your call

Lori L. Dixon, Ed.S.

Dear Reader,

In these days we are living, you have witnessed greater revival than in past days. As you know, we are having powerful challenges and traumas, but we have a God who loves us through it all and in each step we take. Thank you for choosing to read this book and hear the stories of six women who believed and answered the Lord's calling to write for YOU.

You have read the deep stories of faith, loss, joy, healing, surrender, and transformation in the pages of this book. Many of the stories you have read from our women include their testimony of faith, too.

Which ones have touched your heart? Which one

caused you to hear the Holy Spirit speaking to you? Which one aligned with your life circumstance now or even before?

You may be asking, "How do I give my life to Christ and what does that mean?" Are you feeling the nudging of the Holy Spirit to accept Christ into your life and into your heart? There is no age, time, place or certain words to say in this interaction with the Lord. It all begins with a simple understanding and a prayer of acceptance and surrendering of your life to Him. You receive the ability to see clearer the wisdom God gave you back in the Garden of Eden and to begin communing with Him again. You also open the door to letting Christ into your heart where He will never leave. He lives inside of us and walks with us every day.

Declaration

Begin by saying something like, "I believe in God the Father and in Jesus Christ, His Son. I am ready to begin a walk of faith today. I am inviting Christ into my heart."

> For everyone who calls on the name of the Lord will be saved.
>
> Romans 10:13, TPT

Prayer of Surrender

Using this as a guide, pray with a sincere heart:

Dear Father God, I come before You today with a heart filled with faith and love. I surrender my life—all of it, to You. I believe Jesus Christ was born free of sin, died on the cross for me and my sins, and rose from the grave three days later, I believe in Your beautiful gift of salvation, grace, and eternal life because of the sacrifice of Jesus Christ.

Lord, today I repent and turn from my old life. Your grace and mercy bring me to begin walking with a childlike faith. Today, in this moment, I ask you for a new life in which Jesus Christ and the Holy Spirit are within me. Thank you, God, for forgiving me and wiping away my sin away to become brand new in You.

In Jesus' Holy and precious name, Amen.

There is so much I want to share with you about this new walk of faith and how YOU become a sister or brother in the family of God. We are His children.

Will you choose to be a part of the family? We can't wait to greet you and walk with you. You may choose to reach out to one of the authors or to one of us in the WoW Team. We would also love for you to join our Facebook community called, "Wisdom on the Walk Author community" and share your testimony with us. We also have events and prayer team zoom calls together as a community of Christian women. Being with others on this journey is important.

I suggest a few that I love below. Then, begin reading the scriptures shared with you in each of the chapters. Open your heart and let God speak truth into your life… today.

You may want to reach out and obtain the new JOY journal. It is also available on Amazon.

- **King James Version (KJV):** Great for memorizing verses

- **New International Version (NIV):** Easier to read in everyday language

- **The Passion Translation (TPT):** My favorite for connection to your life and sharing with others; only in New Testament, Proverbs, and Psalms at this time, with smaller books just for the Old Testament

If you prayed this prayer and asked Christ into your heart, please reach out to us. We want to pray for you and invite you to join us in our retreats, prayer team, bible studies, and more.

come closer

The Women Behind the Words

Lori L. Dixon, Ed.S.

Have you read their stories yet? Or maybe… you found yourself turning these pages first—curious about the women behind the words.

However you arrived here, it matters that you did.

Because if I could personally invite you into a conversation with each author in this book—I would. I would pull up a chair, pour something warm, and let you hear their hearts the way I have.

Each woman visualized YOU, sitting down for coffee or tea and sharing their intimate and personal story with you.

These are not just writers. They are faith-filled, Christ-centered, Spirit-led, God-directed, purpose-driven women—who said *yes* to sharing pieces of their lives so that yours might be forever changed. Why? Because they care about your walk with God.

Because they understand that one moment—one encounter, one story, one surrendered yes—can become a pivotal turning point in a life.

And so they write not *at* you… but *with* you. As real women. Living real lives. Walking through moments that matter.

Each one has prayed and asked God, *"Which part of my story will serve your Kingdom the most?"*

And what you now hold in your hands… is their answer. I truly cannot wait for you to meet them.

"Meet the Authors" has always felt a bit… stiff to me. A little too formal. A little too distant. Because if you haven't felt it yet—you will.

These women are not simply contributors to a book. They are my sisters. Sisters in faith. Sisters in Christ. Sisters in courage, in calling, in showing up when it would have been easier to stay hidden.

Yes, they are co-authors—but even that feels too small, too labeled for what we've built together.

We are connected through something deeper: through writing, through growth, through obedience, and through a shared desire to see God move in the lives of others.

In 2023, God asked me to write again. And you may already know—He didn't just call me. He called twelve women to come alongside this vision.

Together, we built more than a book. We built an academy. A community. A retreat space for women to grow in transformational writing, editing, visibility, and purpose-driven business.

But more than anything… We built a place where women could encounter God in their story. For many of us, it became a journey of faith that stretched far beyond the page. And the calling didn't stop there. God made it clear—this was only the beginning.

He placed a continued assignment on my life to keep building, keep writing, keep creating space for women to rise and release what He has placed within them for His Kingdom.

And if I'm honest… There are still days I feel a bit like Noah. Building something I can't fully see. Trusting instructions I didn't write. Wondering who will come, how it will unfold, and what impact it will truly have. But choosing obedience anyway.

Our newest book in the series, *Delighting in the Wisdom on the Walk*, introduces a new group of SIX authors—who are new, excited, focused, and Jesus-filled.

And all I can say is this: God is so very good.

What began as a step of faith has grown into something far greater than we imagined. Our monthly WoW Academy has expanded. The offerings have deepened. The sisterhood has strengthened. And the impact? It continues to multiply and ripple out to the women called and committed.

For this group's "induction" into WoW, God led us to begin differently. We started with our online Zoom meetings filled with information. Yet, the connection needed to be deeper. We held our first Masterclass for our authors and opened it up for others who were called.

It was called, "Captured in HIS Presence: Media + Marketing" and we included a full day itinerary with even an exclusive photo shoot. What a day! Held in the Dallas area, on a Saturday, twelve women gathered with intention. Three collaborative partners spearheaded a day of connection and dreaming with vision. God was "surely in this place."

They came to learn. To connect. To write. To listen. But more than anything… they came to respond to God. They were invited into something deeper—to step into their faith walk in a new way, and to answer the call to share their stories of healing, freedom, and transformation through Christ. And they said YES … AND.

These women have done more than write chapters. They have grown together. They have stretched. They have supported one another through life, family, business, and calling. They have faced fears. Broken through limitations. Released old identities. They have laughed at who they used to be… and praised God for who they are becoming.

And they did not do it alone.

WE Share THIS Gentle Invitation

And maybe… as you've been reading, you've felt something stirring. A quiet nudge. A whisper that says, *There's something in me too.*" Perhaps there is a story you've carried. A testimony you've lived. A season God has walked you through that was never meant to stay hidden.

You don't have to have it all figured out. You don't have to feel ready. None of us did. But what if your "yes" could be the very thing God uses to bring healing, freedom, or hope to someone else?

What if the words you've been holding… are meant to be released? Just something to pray about.

On the pages that follow, you will find the biographies of these remarkable women. But don't just read them. **Meet them. Celebrate them. Listen for the heart behind their words. And allow yourself to feel connected to their journey.** Because you will be. And I promise you this: you will be better for it.

I know I am.

If you feel stirred… if something within you is whispering, *"There's more for me too"*—we would love to connect with you. For books, authoring opportunities, or upcoming events, reach out at **lori@walkwithlori.com** or visit **www.walkwithlori.com**.

Be Blessed. Be Bold. Be YOU!

Lori

—Lori and the LLD Legacy Publishing Team

elise anthony

ELISE ANTHONY lives to share the Word of God. She is the founder and publisher of Joy + Gladness, a media company that provides radical encouragement for the soul.

As a former newspaper, magazine, and digital editor, she brings a friend's empathy, a storyteller's curiosity, and a deep love for scripture to her writing.

Whether it's a random act of Joy + Gladness, a devotional, or even a hunt for vintage goodies, Elise spreads joy—with honesty, grace, and sometimes a little laughter—and she hopes her words help readers realize how much they are loved by God and that they indeed each have a divine purpose.

Instagram: @presspass

jennifer luna

JENNIFER LUNA is living proof that broken chapters can become powerful testimonies. Once a quiet underdog shaped by difficult paths and shattered dreams, she's been wrestling with self-worth and had to face the painful truth that she didn't know how to love herself. When everything she had hoped for crumbled and fell apart, she didn't know where to turn, in that instant, she felt Jesus's love and looked to the heavens—and found not condemnation, but calling. Through faith, healing, and courage, Jennifer is reclaiming her voice.

Today she stands resilient and unapologetic, writing to reach beings who have ever felt unseen, unheard, or alone.

Her first book is more than a story—it's a declaration. There is still grace. There is still growth for the ones who truly know God's obedience.

Her message shines bright: God knows both the beginning and the end. Even in your darkest moments, remember—they are not the final chapter. Trust in Jesus' love and courageously write your story.

Facebook: @33Jluna

emily schwindler

EMILY SCHWINDLER is a death educator, Certified Thanatologist, founder of Thanatos Ink, wife, and mother of two. She is the Director of Operations and Engagement, Aaron-Ruben-Nelson Mortuary.

Her background growing up in a small Indiana town, earning a bachelor's in English with a literature concentration and master's certificate in Thanatology give her a unique window into the world.

Emily began working at a funeral home in 2007 and has spent most of her career in deathcare. Over the decades, she has continued expanding her knowledge of burial and cremation, death practice of different religions and cultures, and all things mortuary and grief related. As a result, she is a highly regarded subject matter expert and public speaker in her community. Emily's faith and empathy make her a natural fit for a job most admit they couldn't do.

Her individual approach and genuine kindness are exemplified in the loving care she shows the dead and patient guidance she shows the living.

Email: emily@arnmortuary.com

Instagram: www.instagram.com/emily_schwindler

dorothea shields

DOROTHEA SHIELDS is a Bible teacher, speaker, and author who has spent more than two decades helping women fall more deeply in love with God and His Word. She has a gift for making Scripture simple, relatable, and alive — whether she's teaching from a stage, writing a Bible study, or mentoring women one-on-one.

She is the author of *Fitted for Grace* and *Surrendered: The Life, Ministry, and Journeys of the Apostle Paul*, and contributor to *Delighting in Wisdom on the Walk*.

When she's not teaching or writing, you might find her on a cruise somewhere, ordering hot chocolate for the whipped cream, or tending to her ever-growing collection of plants she unintentionally acquired. She lives in the Dallas, Texas area with her husband, and is a proud mom and Mimi.

Facebook: Dorothea Shields
Facebook Bible Study Group: The Word and Me
Instagram: dorothealshields
You Tube: Dorothea Shields Anchored To Jesus
Email: hello@dorotheashields.com
Website: www.dorotheashields.com
LinkedIn: Dorothea Shields

dr. lynnette simm

DR. LYNNETTE SIMM is a psychologist, educator, author, speaker, and life mentor whose work integrates clinical insight, personal resilience, and deep Christian faith to help others overcome trauma and find restoration.

Holding degrees in Psychology and a Doctorate in Educational Leadership, along with certifications in Adult Training, Learning, and Development, Dr. Simm served as a college professor for more than 15 years at institutions including Pikes Peak College, Regis Jesuit University, and Colorado Christian University. Her academic background informs her compassionate, evidence-based approach to healing.

In 2016, Dr. Simm published her memoir, *And the Day Came*, a raw and faith-centered account of her journey from childhood abandonment and sexual abuse to complete restoration. The book traces her path from a silenced young girl, through therapeutic work that helped her confront buried pain, to a profound spiritual surrender in which she released control to God and embraced Jesus Christ as the source of her worthiness. Themes of breaking silence, radical forgiveness, relational healing, and resilient hope run throughout the memoir and its companion documentary, *Tear-Stained Forgiveness*, which shares her family's redemptive story. Readers and endorsers describe the book as heart-wrenching yet deeply hopeful, highlighting the courage required to expose painful secrets and the reality that "nothing is unforgivable."

After moving to Texas, Dr. Simm collaborated with Michele Hoffman on the memoir and became actively involved in women's ministry. She worked with Pearls Promised Ministries, co-hosting the radio and television show *Pop Talk* alongside Dr. Lisa Worley and Rosemary Legrand to encourage and support women. She has spoken nationally with organizations such as StoneCroft, Becoming Free (a sexual trauma retreat), and contributed to the Roaring Lambs series. She is a founding member of the Dallas Dream Team, which supports faith-based nonprofits in the DFW area, and has served with Ladies In Touch, facilitating community outreach through shared testimonies.

Today, Dr. Lynnette Simm maintains a private practice as a life mentor, guiding young women and married couples as they process past trauma and step into their future. She also serves as Director of Mentorship for Alive at Last Ministries, where she trains volunteers to mentor women and shelter residents in the DFW area who have experienced sexual trauma, exploitation, or trafficking. Her work continues to reflect the central message of her memoir: that therapy, community, and surrendered faith can transform profound brokenness into abundant life and purposeful service.

Throughout her journey, Dr. Simm has been supported by her husband of over 30 years, Madison, their daughters MacKenzie and Alexandra, her extended HuGGS family, and her beloved dogs Theodore and Franklin. She has walked with her Lord and Savior, Jesus Christ, for more than 20 years and anchors her life in Philippians 4:13: "I can do all things through Christ who strengthens me."

Facebook: @lynnette.greshamsimm

Instagram: @drlsimm

connie wallace

CONNIE J. WALLACE is a first-time author and native Texan. After living in Southern California and Atlanta, Georgia through her husband, Doug's career, she returned home to Texas in 2012. Connie spent many years as a devoted caregiver to her parents and in-laws until their passing between 2014 and 2022. She is the proud mother of two sons, Austin and Colton. Connie and Doug live in Corsicana, Texas, next door to Austin, his wife Heather, and their three beautiful children—Finley, Stellan, and Remi. Colton lives with Jesus, in his heavenly home. Connie is a foodie—looks forward to every meal! She enjoys traveling, singing, and spending time with family and friends.

Facebook and Instagram:

@ceejaywallace

A Life Changed
By Christ

Wisdom on the Walk (WoW) book series, academy, and community!

Spirit-filled, Christ-centered, God-directed Life Stories

Has God specifically chosen YOU to be part of a new project to bring forth God's purpose in our lives? YOU are invited to join us in next book in the WoW book series, as we share stories in this meaningful way. It is more than a book; it is an interactive journey of reflection, creativity, learning, connecting, and embracing God's work in your life to influence and impact others. Your story will be intertwined with the writing of best-selling Lori L. Dixon, designs to engage you in furthering your purpose, and areas to reflect on His word in your own life.

I love how God has designed the expansion with further books, an academy of learning and writing, and an online community for sisterhood. What a beautiful and meaningful way to further HIS Kingdom by creating circles of disciples for unique and powerful purposes. As you will experience, we have workshops, prayer team circles, retreats, partners in writing, and engage in time together, sharing information, stories, insights, support, faith, and growth moments.

Welcome to the Wisdom on the Walk Author Journey!

Here are some quick items to know about the experience:

- We meet monthly for 9-12 months.
- Each session includes mentoring, learning, connection, interaction with other authors, bible study, and prayer. You will also have a 1:1 coaching session each month for guidance and direction in your writing, faith walk, social media presence, marketing, media, and more!
- Upcoming retreats in Dallas and beyond are planned for 2024 already.
- Further opportunities for sponsoring, speaking, and writing your own book are available.

Meet our LLD Legacy Publishing and Media Team:

Lori Dixon
owner, author, and your visionary leader in the process

Niki Banning
best-selling author, assistant, and leading editor

Callie Revell
publishing assistant, graphic design, and support

Do you hear that? A call to action. Are you feeling God is calling YOU? Have you ever thought He wants you to share your life story, healing, transformation, and insights with other women and glorify His work in YOU?

Your Story **is waiting to be told.**

Contact us for more information about the WoW Journey or to publish your book with us!

meet Lori L. Dixon

@walkwithlori
@lorilanedixon

Lori L. Dixon, Ed.S. is a Visionary and Epiphany Expert with her business ventures, LLD Legacy Publishing, LLC, and Walk with Lori. Lori brings more than 4 decades of wisdom and experience working in education, therapies, business, and nonprofits. She is a best-selling author and publisher, thera-coach, speaker, and a multiple international award-winning host and producer on TV. With her dynamic television appearances on Bravo's Real Housewives of Dallas, Lori understands the 'reality' of how the next chapter of life may be rewritten at any time. She may now be watched internationally on TV as a co-host on Lite It Up TV and Sawubona...I SEE You on ZondraTV Network on ROKU, AmazonFire, Chromecast, and iTunes.

Lori believes in finding the "heartstrings" in life, releasing the strongholds of fear, and living the life God has designed for you. As a writer for many years and a published author, editor, and frequent media influencer for others, Lori knew her passion would always be in the "stories" of our lives. She expanded her mission for writing and publishing with her own Christ-centered, faith-filled books, numerous compilations, and children's books. Lori believes we are all SEEN in our own God-given divine design and that we have a mission to share it right now within the world.

Through LLD Legacy Publishing, LLC, which is a full-service publishing company with editing, writing, illustrating, design, media, and marketing, she brings her passions together for each author. Her newest program, Wisdom on the Walk (WoW) is a unique experiential journey for women to become authors and further their own stories and missions for others.

LORI L. DIXON, Ed.S.

Founder and Owner, LLD Legacy and Walk with Lori

TheraCoach, Publisher
International Multiple Award-Winning Host and Producer

469-855-0287
www.walkwithlori.com
lori@walkwithlori.com

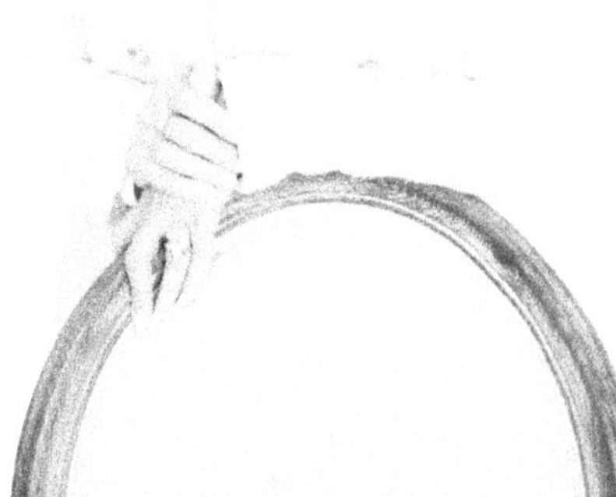

Did you gain wisdom on your walk?
Order more copies to pour into others!

www.walkwithlori.com/wisdomonwalk

or scan this code with your phone: